Who Wins in a Digital World?

**The Digital Future of Management Series from
MIT Sloan Management Review**

Paul Michelman, series editor

How to Go Digital: Practical Wisdom to Help Drive Your Organization's Digital Transformation

What the Digital Future Holds: 20 Groundbreaking Essays on How Technology Is Reshaping the Practice of Management

When Innovation Moves at Digital Speed: Strategies and Tactics to Provoke, Sustain, and Defend Innovation in Today's Unsettled Markets

Who Wins in a Digital World? Strategies to Make Your Organization Fit for the Future

Who Wins in a Digital World?

Strategies to Make Your Organization Fit for the Future

MIT Sloan Management Review

The MIT Press
Cambridge, Massachusetts
London, England

This book was set in Stone Serif and Neue Haas Grotesk Text by Jen Jackowitz. Printed and bound in the United States of America.

Library of Congress Cataloging-in-Publication Data

Names: MIT Sloan Management Review, compiler.
Title: Who wins in a digital world? : strategies to make your organization
    fit for the future / MIT Sloan Management Review.
Description: Cambridge, MA : MIT Press, [2019] | Series: The digital future
    of management | Includes bibliographical references and index.
Identifiers: LCCN 2018034414 | ISBN 9780262536745 (pbk. : alk. paper)
Subjects: LCSH: Internet--Social aspects. | Information technology--Social
    aspects.
Classification: LCC HM851 .W4558 2019 | DDC 302.23/1--dc23 LC record
available at https://lccn.loc.gov/2018034414

10   9   8   7   6   5   4   3   2   1

Contents

Series Foreword

Books in the Digital Future of Management series draw from the print and web pages of MIT Sloan Management Review to deliver expert insights and sharply tuned advice on navigating the unprecedented challenges of the digital world. These books are essential reading for executives from the world's leading source of ideas on how technology is transforming the practice of management.

Paul Michelman
Editor in Chief
MIT Sloan Management Review

Introduction: Who Wins in a Digital World?

Paul Michelman

Is your organization building the capabilities it will need to survive and thrive in a digital world?

This may be *the* question of the moment for business leaders. It's certainly the question that will separate the companies that will prosper in this new world from those that will struggle or fail.

Adapting a company to capitalize on the full potential of digital technologies and fend off the swarms of new competitors they enable requires a compelling vision—a tangible and engaging view of the future that people can believe in. Creating that vision requires identifying what success will look like in this new world and how your company can reach its goals while moving toward new definitions of achievement.

We live in a world where the unknowns are never-ending; thus, our ability to embrace the demands of change has become a prerequisite for success. This is true at both the individual level—for each of us as professionals—and at the organizational level—for the companies and institutions that we lead and work within.

Change is not executed by a vision; it is executed by individuals. No matter how smart the strategy and how well articulated the plan, only people can bring about actual change.

Given this reality, what strategies will it take to keep pace in today's environment, one in which individuals and businesses are expected to pivot repeatedly toward new ways of working?

I think of this challenge along three dimensions:

- The ability to be both flexible and focused
- The ability to evolve and to embrace all the messiness therein
- The ability to move and adapt quickly

In this book, we've collected some of the best new thinking and research on these three topics. The authors draw insights and advice from real-world examples of how new companies are emerging from the digital soup and how legacy organizations are making the transition from the old ways of working to the new.

In part I, we dive into the need for adaptability. In a changing world, an organization's capabilities are no longer just about what is required to be successful today. Instead, organizations, like people, need the ability to excel in what their roles *will become* as their competitive ecosystems evolve. Is your organization able to adopt new tools and strategies to succeed in the digital arena?

In this section, we present four big-picture themes:

- **Don't Confuse Digital with Digitization.** Jeanne Ross (MIT Sloan School of Management's Center for Information Systems Research) argues that digitization is an important enabler of digital but won't transform a business into a digital company on its own. Instead, companies must rethink their value propositions and focus on delivering a seamless, digitally enabled customer experience.

- **Is Your Company Ready for a Digital Future?** Peter Weill and Stephanie L. Woerner (both of MIT's Center for Information Systems Research) lay out four pathways that businesses can take to become top performers in the digital economy, noting that leadership's role is to determine which pathway to pursue—and how aggressively to move.

- **Turn Strategy into Results.** Donald Sull (MIT Sloan School of Management), Stefano Turconi (London Business School), Charles Sull (Charles Thames Strategy Partners), and James Yoder (formerly of Charles Thames) examine how leaders can translate the complexity of strategy into guidelines that are simple and flexible enough to execute. They advocate for developing a small set of priorities rather than trying to boil down strategy to a pithy statement.

- **Leading in a Time of Increased Expectations.** In a Q&A, Lynn J. Good, CEO of Duke Energy, talks about how big energy companies, which have traditionally focused solely on power generation, are increasingly becoming customer-centric. It's a change brought on by digitally empowered customers who are vocal about everything from where their energy should originate to when their bills should arrive.

In part II, we explore the need for nerve. Does your organization have the appetite—and desire and tenacity—to evolve and try new things? Is it legitimately interested in charting a new future?

In this section, we highlight specific strategies and mindsets:

- **Don't Get Caught in the Middle.** In this essay, I note that while there was once a time when middlemen were indispensable, technology is rendering such intermediaries obsolete. The real worth is increasingly found at the extremes of value chains and organizations, not at the center.

- **The Best Response to Digital Disruption.** Jacques Bughin (McKinsey & Co.) and Nicolas van Zeebroeck (Solvay Brussels School of Economics and Management) explore why companies that adopt bold strategies in the face of industry digitization improve their odds of coming out winners.

- **Why Your Company Needs More Collaboration.** My *MIT Sloan Management Review* colleague David Kiron draws from three separate research projects that *MIT SMR* conducted over three years for his finding that digitization demands an unprecedented focus on cooperation and collaboration.

- **What's Your Cognitive Technology Strategy?** Thomas H. Davenport (Babson College) and Vikram Mahidhar (Genpact) note that, for many leaders, artificial intelligence and cognitive technologies are the most disruptive forces on the horizon. But most organizations still are looking for a strategy to address them.

In part III, we explore the need for speed. Change usually requires a new speed—a higher gear than individuals and organizations are accustomed to. And this pace won't let up: Digital life moves faster. Can your organization shift gears to keep up?

Some might argue that a focus on velocity can be counterproductive—that amid all this digital turmoil, considered decision making is more important than ever. I believe that is a false argument. You must be able to move quickly *and* make smart bets at the same time.

In this section, we lay out the best strategies for moving fast:

- **Building a More Intelligent Enterprise.** Paul J. H. Schoemaker (formerly of the Mack Center for Technological Innovation at the Wharton School) and Philip E. Tetlock (University of Pennsylvania) examine how managers can combine human intelligence with technology-enabled insights to make smarter choices in the face of uncertainty and complexity.

- **Creating Management Processes Built for Change.** Christopher G. Worley (NEOMA Business School), Thomas Williams (independent management consultant), and Edward E. Lawler III (University of Southern California) lay out the ways that agile management processes can help organizations change.

- **Building the Right Ecosystem for Innovation.** Nathan Furr and Andrew Shipilov (both of INSEAD) discuss why, as companies grapple with uncertainty and change, they must collaborate in new ways with unlikely partners.

- **Implement First, Ask Questions Later (or Not at All).** Stephen J. Andriole (Villanova School of Business) explains that today's inexpensive cloud-based apps mean that emerging technology is piloted and adopted before its business requirements are understood—and there's no going back to the old, leisurely days.

Thinking along the three dimensions we outline in this book will make the challenges of change—especially ongoing change—more tangible.

But that's not enough.

We should all ask ourselves hard questions as we consider the inevitable transformations of our industries, our organizations, and our individual places in the digital world. Ask yourself: Am I up for this, as a leader and as a participant? Can I do what it takes to succeed in a continually evolving environment? *Will I?*

The kind of transformation we are experiencing in business today isn't easy for anyone. We don't work the way we did last year. Next year, we'll work and compete differently again. If your organization doesn't embrace the realities and requirements of change, you need to understand that it will be under siege from those that do.

At the same time, I believe there's great energy and possibility in all this. Once you accept the truth that change is ongoing, change becomes more about opportunity and less about challenge. If you have the flexibility, the will to evolve, and the courage to shift up, change becomes stimulating, and exhilarating, and something to be embraced. We hope this book will help get you to that point.

1
Be Flexible. Keep Focused.

1

Don't Confuse Digital with Digitization

Jeanne Ross

Digitization involves standardizing business processes and is associated with cost cutting and operational excellence. In essence, it imposes discipline on business processes that, over the years, were executed by individual heroes in a variety of creative (but not always optimal) ways. SAP, PeopleSoft, and other integrated software packages that burst onto the scene in the 1990s helped lead the way into more digitizing, but it remains a painful process.

Today, companies are confronting something new and different: digital. Digital, of course, is an adjective. It refers to a host of powerful, accessible, and potentially game-changing technologies like social, mobile, cloud, analytics, internet of things, cognitive computing, and biometrics. It also refers to the transformation that companies must undergo to take advantage of the opportunities these technologies create. A digital transformation involves rethinking the company's value proposition, not just its operations. A digital company innovates to deliver enhanced products, services, and customer engagement. Digital is exciting, thrilling—and a bit unnerving!

The problem is this: We have found that many business leaders are thinking of digital as advanced digitization, such as enhancing the customer experience with mobile technologies or implementing internet of things capabilities to improve operations. But "becoming digital" is a totally different exercise from digitizing. Companies today must become digital to compete in a world in which both end consumers and business customers expect products and services to meet their needs on demand across channels. In most industries, digital is already a business imperative. Digitization is an important enabler of digital, but all the digitization in the world won't, on its own, make a business a digital company. I would argue, in fact, that failing to distinguish increased digitization (even radically increased digitization) from a digital transformation could be a fatal mistake.

Digitization Is an Operational Necessity

The benefits of digitization are significant: efficiency, operational excellence, predictability. For all the pain that it entails, digitization is an essential undertaking in companies. Without digitization, companies cannot scale; they cannot absorb the complexity of expanded product portfolios; they cannot personalize services. Disciplined, standardized business processes, where appropriate, ensure the accuracy and security of core transactions and back-office processes. They make data accessible and reliable.

Most companies have grossly underestimated the challenge of digitization. Shedding habits—imposing discipline—has proved to be harder than business leaders imagined. In many cases, leaders have committed to digitization initiatives thinking they are funding new and better technology. Many didn't recognize that digitization requires a commitment to fundamental changes in how people work. Consequently, most digitization efforts cost more—and generate fewer benefits—than anticipated.

MIT Sloan School of Management's Center for Information Systems Research (CISR) has found that only 28% of established companies have successfully digitized, despite more than 20 years of business digitization history. This is a problem, because companies must be digitized if they hope to become digital. Without digitization, management's attention will be consumed with fixing whatever is going wrong today in a company's operations. There will be no time for innovation. Leaders won't have the resources to invest in a digital transformation or the operational excellence to support their digital value proposition.

Digital Is a Customer-Centric Value Proposition

To become digital, leaders must articulate a visionary digital value proposition. This value proposition must reassess how digital technologies and information can enhance an organization's existing assets and capabilities to create new customer value. Being digital is not just introducing mobile apps for customers. It is taking advantage of the opportunity to redefine a business—and possibly even an industry.

Big, established companies have started to define visionary digital value propositions. Schneider Electric, headquartered in France, has moved beyond selling electrical products to providing energy management solutions. California-based managed care consortium Kaiser Permanente views itself not as a health care provider but as a patient-provider collaboration. BMW is not just an automobile manufacturer; it's a provider of "individual mobility." Netherlands-based Philips has sold off multiple businesses, including its foundational lighting business, to focus on "improving lives through health care innovation."

These are bold strokes. They are risky. But the alternative is to try to succeed in a digital economy with a predigital value proposition. That could be the riskiest alternative of all.

To become digital and pursue a digital vision, companies must define their digital offerings. They must embrace information-enriched customer solutions delivered as a seamless, personalized customer experience. Digital offerings are the specific solutions that deliver on a company's digital value proposition. The benefits of a successful digital transformation include growth in revenues and margins, undying customer loyalty, and the ability to attract top talent (and thus continue to grow).

Successful companies in the digital economy will be digital (to provide customer value) and digitized (to provide for scale and efficiency). Although companies still struggle to digitize, what it means and how to do it are now well-established. It's just hard to do well. How to be digital, in contrast, is less well-established. Defining a value proposition that will attract customers who are actually willing to pay for a given solution is more art than science.

Five Guiding Principles for a Digital Transformation

If you want to get started on a digital transformation, I suggest you embrace five guiding principles:

- **Don't hand off responsibility for your digital transformation to your information technology (IT) unit.** This is a business transformation. If you think IT can make it happen, the game is over!
- **Do engage IT leaders in defining your vision and mapping your initiatives.** Your embedded culture and structures will

be your two biggest obstacles to your digital transformation, but your legacy IT systems are more likely a liability than an asset. IT leaders can help establish what's possible.

- **Bring in professional help.** You wouldn't add a room to your house without consulting an architect, so make sure you understand that in trying to coordinate the business components, roles, structures, processes, and systems that will enable you to deliver digital offerings, you need professional business architects. Stop thinking of architecture as an IT issue, and engage in developing your business architecture.

- **Be persistent and patient.** Understand that you will need to invest time and money in your digital initiatives, just like venture capital companies invest in innovative businesses. The cost savings from digitization were easy to track. The new revenues from digital initiatives probably won't flow in quickly. Track some intermediate metrics like reuse and time to market.

- **Prepare to co-create with customers.** Unless you have Apple cofounder Steve Jobs's gift for anticipating what customers want, you'll need to engage them in the process of defining your offerings. Otherwise, you may never see those new revenues you're counting on.

It will take time to settle on a pattern of digital offerings that bring value to your customers and your business. It will take even longer to identify, build, and reuse business components so that new solutions can be easily configured. And for many companies, there is still much work to be done to ensure that they are sufficiently digitized to support a digital transformation.

In short, your digital transformation will be a long journey. It's important to get started.

2

Is Your Company Ready for a Digital Future?

Peter Weill and Stephanie L. Woerner

In preparing for the future, many large, established enterprises are embarking on a digital business transformation journey—often without any sense of where they are going. In this article, we will present four viable pathways for transformation and examine their pros and cons. However, the goal isn't digital transformation but rather *business* transformation—using digital capabilities to transform a traditional enterprise into a top performer in the digital economy. We call such top-performing enterprises "future-ready."

In 2015 and 2017, we surveyed several hundred enterprises,[1] examining both the capabilities needed for transformation and the impacts on performance. We also had conversations with more than 50 executives to learn about their experiences with digital business transformation. Respondents represented a wide variety of industries, with manufacturing, financial services, and IT software and services being the biggest groups. Based on our analysis, future-ready enterprises performed much better than their industry peers. But we also found that, even within a single industry, enterprises can take different paths to becoming future-ready. This article looks at four banks that have taken different pathways: Danske Bank, mBank, BBVA, and ING.

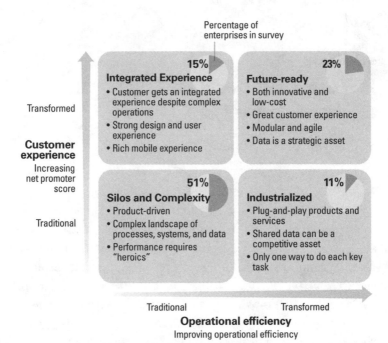

Percentage of enterprises in survey

15%
Integrated Experience
- Customer gets an integrated experience despite complex operations
- Strong design and user experience
- Rich mobile experience

23%
Future-ready
- Both innovative and low-cost
- Great customer experience
- Modular and agile
- Data is a strategic asset

51%
Silos and Complexity
- Product-driven
- Complex landscape of processes, systems, and data
- Performance requires "heroics"

11%
Industrialized
- Plug-and-play products and services
- Shared data can be a competitive asset
- Only one way to do each key task

Transformed

Customer experience
Increasing net promoter score

Traditional

Traditional   Transformed
Operational efficiency
Improving operational efficiency

How Companies Compare on Digital Business Transformation

In 2015 and 2017, we surveyed several hundred enterprises, examining both the capabilities needed for transformation and the impacts on performance. Based on our analysis, companies in the future-ready quadrant performed much better than their industry peers. Becoming future-ready requires changing the enterprise on two dimensions—customer experience and operational efficiency. We found that enterprises can take one of four different paths to go from the lower-left quadrant (Silos and Complexity) to the upper-right (Future-ready).

Becoming Future-Ready

Becoming future-ready requires changing the enterprise on two dimensions—customer experience and operational efficiency.

Future-Ready

Future-ready enterprises are able to innovate to engage and satisfy customers while at the same time reducing costs. Their goal is to meet customers' needs rather than push products, and customers can expect to have a good experience no matter which service delivery channel they choose. On the operations side, the company's capabilities are modular and agile; data is a strategic asset that is shared and accessible to all those in the company who need it. The enterprise is ready to compete in the digital economy and able to work with a wide variety of partners through both digital services and exposed application programming interfaces (APIs). By these criteria, 23% of the businesses we surveyed were future-ready, shown in the upper-right quadrant of the exhibit. Their performance averaged 16 percentage points better than their industry average, meaning that if the average net profit margin for a company in a given industry was 8%, future-ready enterprises earned 24%.

Silos and Complexity

Of the companies we surveyed, 51% were in the bottom-left quadrant, with an extensive catalog of products and services developed over many years. Their products and services are supported by a complex set of business processes, systems, and data. The result is a fragmented, labor-intensive, and frustrating customer experience, often made worse by product silos within the company.

Frequently, the ability of such organizations to provide an engaging customer experience depends heavily on heroics by employees. For example, we watched one bank teller work with an elderly customer who wanted to change her address on six different bank products. The number of keystrokes required to make the necessary changes was dizzying. During a 20-minute encounter, the teller chatted amiably with the customer about the local sports team. An amazing effort, to be sure—but not scalable. It shouldn't be surprising that, in our survey, the profit margins of enterprises from this group were weak; they averaged 5 percentage points below their industry average.

Industrialized

Companies characterized by digital industrialization, shown in the bottom-right quadrant, apply the best practices of automation to their operations. They use the features that make them strong as an enterprise and turn them into modular and standardized digitized services. For example, companies in this group picked the best way of handling each key task (processing an insurance claim, on-boarding a customer, or assessing risk) and deployed it across the enterprise. They configured their services into plug-and-play modules to meet particular customer requirements quickly and inexpensively. The consolidated data created from the customer interactions and operations can become a competitive asset that anyone involved in the enterprise can access. Over time, many of these processes and decisions can be automated. Of the companies we studied, 11% were in the industrialized group; their net profit margins averaged 4.6 percentage points higher than their industry average.

Integrated Experience

Enterprises offering what we call an "integrated experience," shown in the upper-left quadrant, provide a better-than-industry-average customer experience despite having complex operations. Some of the companies emulated the industry-leading model epitomized by United Services Automobile Association (USAA), the San Antonio, Texas-based financial services group. USAA is organized around addressing a customer's life events (for example, buying a house, having a baby, or preparing for retirement) rather than pushing products. We have seen companies that want to offer an integrated experience develop attractive websites and mobile apps and hire more relationship managers to improve the customer experience. Many attempt to improve the customer experience by investing in analytics. However, we have found that these enterprises typically are unable to simplify or automate the underlying and complex business processes, technology, and data landscape. As a result, they see their costs of serving customers increase. About 15% of enterprises we studied offered an integrated experience; their net profit margins averaged 3.6 percentage points below their industry average.

Four Pathways to Transformation

We identified four different pathways that companies took to become future-ready. Each pathway begins in the bottom-left quadrant (Silos and Complexity), and each involves significant organizational disruption.

Pathway 1: Standardize first   Pathway 1 moves enterprises from the Silos and Complexity quadrant to the Industrialized quadrant. This pathway relies on building a platform mindset with API-enabled business services that can be accessed across the enterprise and also externally. It enables an organization to eliminate many of its legacy processes and systems. But, as anyone who's been through an enterprise resource planning, customer relationship management, or core banking project will attest, replacing core processes in an enterprise is an expensive, multiyear undertaking. It also requires putting many other projects on hold. Cloud computing, APIs, micro services, and better solution architectures make this industrialization process quicker, less risky, and less disruptive.[2] However, embarking on Pathway 1 takes time. Among other things, it requires changing the decision rights to emphasize integrated services for customers, rather than focusing on products.[3]

Danske Bank A/S, headquartered in Copenhagen, Denmark, and operating in 16 countries, has been pursuing Pathway 1. The vision it presented on its website in 2012 was: "One platform—exceptional brands." Danske Bank's approach brought some early benefits, allowing it to acquire five banks in six years and to reduce operating expenses. In the past few years, Danske Bank has also revamped its financial products into a set of banking services that can be combined to create products in real time across distribution channels in most markets. In the core banking services, 90% of its applications are shared and standardized. At the same time, it simplified its management structure, slimming down its product owner organizations. Whereas there used to be many executives responsible for credit cards, for example, today there's just one.[4]

Danske Bank's "one platform" approach has also delivered longer-term benefits in terms of its relationships with customers and its reputation among peers. In the five years between November 2012 and November 2017, its share price rose approximately 150%. Although the bank cut its number of retail branches by half between 2012 and 2015, it has seen tremendous increases in e-banking. About 2.2 million of its 3.2 million customers use Danske Bank's e-banking platform for such things as paying

Replacing core processes in an enterprise is an expensive, multiyear undertaking. It also requires putting many other projects on hold.

bills, accessing accounts, and managing their retirement savings. Moreover, the bank's payment app, called MobilePay, is so popular that it has been embraced by other Scandinavian banks.[5]

Pathway 2: Improve customer experience first Pathway 2 involves moving from the Silos and Complexity to the Integrated Experience quadrant. Companies choose this strategy when their most pressing strategic goal is to improve the customer experience across the whole enterprise, tackling the problem across multiple organizational silos. Typically, they attempt to do several things at once: develop new attractive offers, build mobile apps and websites, improve call centers, and empower relationship managers—all with the goal of measurably increasing customer satisfaction.

One company following this approach is mBank S.A., headquartered in Warsaw, Poland. The bank's leadership realized back in 2000 that the typical banking customer experience in Poland was far from positive. This led mBank to initiate a series of changes, including opening call centers, offering online services, and adding many new banking products. As it introduced new products and features, it also expanded into new markets in two neighboring countries, the Czech Republic and Slovakia.[6]

Eventually, mBank's leadership concluded that the company's old service platform had reached its limit. Struggling to deliver the desired flexibility and customer experience—and predicting that the problems would only worsen—the bank set out to develop a new banking platform. Created over 14 months, the new platform offers customers a wide range of features, including 30-second loan approvals, mobile payments, video chat, integration with Facebook, peer-to-peer transfers, and cardless ATM withdrawals. The new platform is designed to increase efficiency and reduce time to market. When customers perform transactions or make changes on their mBank mobile app, the information is available immediately to customer representatives and distribution channels.

To grow, mBank has created business channels that tap into its digitized platform, allowing it to offer services to an expanded set of customers via partnerships with other companies. It is thus able to expand the business into new markets or offer its services through noncompeting banks in other countries.

The advantages of Pathway 2 include focusing on the customer first and improving the customer experience, which results in higher customer satisfaction scores and sometimes increased sales. The biggest disadvantage is that the improvements in the customer experience typically add more complexity to already complex systems and processes, increasing the cost to serve a customer. Employees may still need to perform heroics to deliver what was promised.

Pathway 3: Take stair steps   Enterprises on Pathway 3 move toward becoming future-ready by alternating their focus from improving customer experience to improving operations and then back again, shifting the focus back and forth as needed. For example, the first move might be a project to implement an omnichannel experience. After that, companies might improve operations, perhaps by replacing a few legacy processes or creating an API layer. Then, they might attempt to put together a more attractive set of customer offerings by making smarter use of internal data.

With this approach, the difference between success and failure is having a road map that informs everyone's efforts versus taking a haphazard approach. The best way to tell the difference is to ask a manager how a specific project fits into the overall plan. The advantage is that the steps, which consist of tightly coordinated sets of projects, are smaller, reducing risk. The disadvantage is that explaining the intermittent changes in direction can be difficult and can even confuse employees. In some enterprises, we have seen organizational whiplash from changes in direction, with a reduction in employee effectiveness and an increase in burnout.

An example of Pathway 3 can be found in Banco Bilbao Vizcaya Argentaria Sociedad Anonima (BBVA), based in Bilbao, Spain. Responding to challenges he saw in the banking industry, BBVA executive chairman Francisco González announced plans in 2015 to build "the best digital bank of the 21st century."[7] In its effort to reshape the customer experience, BBVA introduced a mobile app in 2014 that offers simple new-customer on-boarding in less than five minutes. It serves as a digital wallet and allows customers to set up appointments and conduct instant messaging conversations with managers. The app also allows easy, automated purchases from a self-service suite of products, including consumer loans and investment funds. The changes have been well-received by bank customers; in early 2017, customers interacted with the bank on average 150 times per year via their mobile devices, compared to four branch visits in the same year.

To improve efficiency, BBVA has worked hard to remove legacy business processes that had been constructed over time from many different systems and versions of data, replacing them with scalable, reusable global digital platforms. Today, BBVA offers customers a digital experience via a reliable core banking platform, enabling new developments that combine the bank's open APIs and other capabilities. A big advantage of this approach is that other enterprises, including retailers, telcos, and even startups, are able to tie into the bank's services, thereby enhancing their own products.

Pathway 4: Create a new organization   Rather than fight an uphill battle to transform their existing organization, leaders who choose to pursue Pathway 4 start new enterprises that begin life as future-ready. In the automobile industry, for example, German carmaker Audi AG recently created a wholly owned subsidiary to develop experimental mobility services apart from car ownership. In banking, ING Groep N.V., the multinational banking and financial services company based in Amsterdam, has pursued a similar approach with ING Direct.

ING launched ING Direct in Canada in 1997 before expanding into Australia, Italy, Spain, the United Kingdom, the United States, and other countries. By 2006, it had 13 million customers in nine countries. Although ING Direct did have some ATMs, it had no branches. Customers interacted with the bank by phone, mail, or online. After beginning as a monoline bank offering high-interest deposit products, it gradually added multiple new products, including loans and mortgages.

ING Direct's country-based businesses operated autonomously but shared a common set of standardized business solutions and technical platform components. Module reuse kept operational costs low, allowing the businesses to offer higher savings rates and lower-cost loans.[8]

It took several years for ING Direct to establish its brand, culture, products, platforms, and partnerships. In our research, we have seen that the big challenge for enterprises taking Pathway 4 is figuring out how to bring the parent company and the transformed enterprise together.

Everything about them—their business models, their cultures, even the customers they cater to—tends to be different. Like every parent of a Pathway 4 enterprise, ING had to figure out how to deal with a successful spin-off. Complicating matters was the fact that there was no single ING Direct; each country operated a little differently. In the face of difficulties following the 2008 financial crisis, ING sold some of its operations, including ING Direct in the United States, Canada, and the United Kingdom,[9] while continuing to hold on to its businesses in other countries, including Australia and Spain. The company says that it plans to standardize on a single digital banking platform by 2021, with data and support functions shared across countries and product lines.[10]

The advantage of Pathway 4 is that it allows an enterprise to build its customer base, people, culture, processes, and systems from scratch to be future-ready. It doesn't need to deal with legacy systems or silos or culture. The challenge is that once the new entity is successful, how do you—or *do* you—integrate it with the mother ship?

Choosing a Pathway

Leadership's role is to determine which pathway the enterprise (or, depending on the circumstances, the business unit) should take and how aggressively to move. Start by determining where the company is today—based on metrics such as net promoter score and net margin—compared to the rest of the industry.

Another important step is selecting the right executive to lead the transformation.[11] The right choice will depend on the company's circumstances, the industry environment, and the direction management wants to go.

- Pathway 1 makes sense if the customer experience the company provides is around industry average and the threat of digital disruption is not high. CIOs are a good choice to lead Pathway 1.

- Pathway 2 makes sense if the customer experience the company provides is significantly worse than average and you can't wait to improve, or if there are worrisome new competitors. An executive passionate about customer experience who is technologically literate is a good choice to lead Pathway 2.

- Pathway 3 makes sense if the customer experience the company provides is a problem, but you can identify a few limited initiatives that will make a big difference. Start with those and then focus on operations—and repeat in small steps. A chief digital officer is a good choice to lead Pathway 3.

- Pathway 4—building a new enterprise—makes sense when you can't see a way to change the culture or the customer experience and operations fast enough to survive. The CEO or COO are good choices to lead Pathway 4.

Once the company—that is, the board, the CEO, and the senior management team—settles on a pathway, the difficult work begins. The digital era is a great opportunity for leaders to reinvent the enterprise. The most successful enterprises will need to become future-ready and ambidextrous—constantly innovating to improve customer experience while also working to reduce costs. Those that don't become future-ready will likely suffer a death by a thousand cuts, with startups, players from other industries, and agile competitors slicing bits out of their businesses.

We conclude on a cautionary but realistic note. We recently ran a workshop on digital business transformation with the CEO and the executive team of an international financial services firm. We asked attendees to plot their company's journey over the previous three years using the pathway framework. After the other executives had presented, we invited the CEO to share his version. He drew a series of movements, beginning in the Silos and Complexity quadrant, moving up, then to the right, then down and back, charting a convoluted path that continued for several more squiggles. When the CEO finished, he stepped back and said, "You know, it's not as if we planned to do it that way. But using the objective metrics against our industry, this is the path we followed."

He concluded by expressing his view that leaders need to pick a pathway and then stick to it. Ultimately, we think this is good advice. After all, transformation is difficult. All of a company's stakeholders—including the board, employees, partners, and customers—need to know where the enterprise is going and how it plans to get there.

3

Turn Strategy into Results

Donald Sull, Stefano Turconi, Charles Sull, and
James Yoder

Strategy, at its heart, is about choice. Few companies succeed by making a single big bet. Most winning strategies are based on a bundle of choices about, among other things, the customers to serve, the scope of the business, product offerings, and capabilities that interact with one another to help a company make money.[1] Consider Trader Joe's Co., the US grocery retailer based in Monrovia, California. Its focus on educated, health-conscious customers influences where it locates its stores, which products it stocks, and the type of employees it hires. The company's choices reinforce one another to increase customers' willingness to pay, reduce its costs, and thereby drive profitability. The dense interdependencies among the choices prevent rivals from imitating Trader Joe's winning strategy. Piecemeal imitation of a few elements—for example, the store format or the focus on private labels—wouldn't work. Instead, a rival would need to replicate the full set of interconnected choices.

Strategy is inherently complex. We see this in the thick reports and complex frameworks that companies use to describe their strategic choices and how these connect with one another. Describing a strategy favors complexity, but executing it requires simplicity. To influence day-to-day activities, strategies need to be simple enough for leaders at every level of the organization to understand, communicate, and remember—a strategy that gathers dust on a shelf is nothing more than an expensive bookend. A strategy for execution must provide concrete guidance while leaving managers with enough flexibility to seize novel opportunities, mitigate unexpected risks, and adapt to local conditions. The act of codifying past choices into an explicit strategy, moreover, reinforces historical commitments and locks a company into inertia.[2] Complex strategies, particularly those that include detailed plans, tend to be long on guidance but short on flexibility.

Strategy Made Simple

How can leaders translate the complexity of strategy into something simple and flexible enough to execute? Your first instinct might be to boil down a complex set of choices to a handful that matter the most. Indeed, a series of strategy experts have argued that managers should do just that by distilling their strategy to a concise statement (fewer than 35 words) summarizing a few core choices.[3] The strategy distillation approach hinges on a few fundamental strategic categories—such as the choice of target customer or core competencies—that can summarize the heart of any company's strategy. The authors illustrate this approach with strategies they have inferred from observing what has worked in the past at successful companies such as Southwest Airlines Co. or Ikea.

We have learned, however, that this approach works best with companies that have relatively straightforward strategies to begin with. Part of our research on strategy execution included a four-year action research project in which we worked with top management teams of eight to 12 companies per year in formulating strategies for execution.[4] The teams used a framework that boiled down their company's strategy to three elements: target customers (who), the value proposition (what), and how the company would deliver, sell, and distribute products or services (how).[5] The approach worked well for a subset of the companies, including a low-cost regional airline, a single-format retailer, a restaurant chain, and a producer of steel girders. Although operating in different industries, the companies shared three characteristics: They focused on a single business, they offered a standard value proposition to a clearly identified customer segment, and their strategy was stable over time.

Executives in companies that didn't fit this mold, by contrast, struggled to boil down their strategy to a few key choices. An online job site in Eastern Europe, for example, could not identify just one target customer because it served job seekers, employers, advertisers, and partners that listed jobs in multiple countries. Leaders elsewhere found it difficult to combine corporate and business-unit strategies into a single formula. One company ran an online high school and a separate division that developed digital content, which it sold to other educational institutions (including other high schools). The two divisions were deeply interwoven, but the leadership team never managed to articulate a single strategy that worked for both parts of the business.

Strategies in transition posed another challenge. Combining choices that drove historical success with those required to win in the future resulted in convoluted statements that left employees baffled as to where they should focus. Simple strategies, we found, don't work for companies that compete in multiple businesses, serve multiple customers, or are in the midst of a strategic transition.

Distilling a strategy into a few core choices sounds great in theory but often derails in practice. You might think the issue was the specific framework we chose, but the roots of the problem go much deeper. To differentiate a company from rivals, the strategy should be specific to the company's history and context, which implies the list of potentially strategic choices is long. Any short list of essential factors is likely to exclude choices that are critical to some companies.[6] To be clear, this critique is not meant to devalue the work of the strategy scholars who created these frameworks but rather to underscore the difficulty of reducing the inherent complexity of strategy into simple statements. Many companies simply cannot cram 10 pounds of strategic complexity into a 3-pound bag.

If boiling down a complex bundle of choices to a few key elements doesn't create a strategy for execution, what does?

Strategic Priorities

Instead of trying to summarize their strategy in a pithy statement, managers should translate it into a handful of actions the company must take to execute that strategy over the medium term. Strategic priorities should be forward-looking and action-oriented and focus attention on the handful of choices that matter most to the organization's success over the next few years.

Many complex organizations that compete across multiple industries, product lines, and customer segments rely on strategic priorities to advance strategy. In the materials we examined from S&P 500 companies, for example, more than two-thirds of the companies published explicit midterm objectives intended to help implement their strategy.

About the Research

The data on prevalence of strategic priorities among large corporations draws on an analysis of how large, publicly traded companies described their strategy in public documents. Our sample consisted of 494 companies included in the 2014 Standard & Poor's 500 Index (S&P 500) that were still publicly traded at the end of 2015. We examined each company's filings with the US Securities and Exchange Commission and other formal communications to investors, and used a five-pronged test to identify strategic priorities: They were presented as an explicit set; they were prioritized; they were expressed as actions; they described how a company planned to execute its strategy; they focused on the midterm (in the range of three years) as opposed to quarterly or annual targets.

We then classified the strategic priorities by topic. To create our initial topics, we focused on four approaches to strategy: dominant logic, market positioning, resources and capabilities, and stakeholder theory. We reviewed the relevant literature to identify concepts commonly associated with each approach to strategy, such as customer intimacy and operational excellence (dominant logic), low price and differentiation (market positioning), brand and intellectual property (resource-based view of strategy), and regulatory compliance (stakeholder theory). We independently hand-coded 500 strategic priorities selected at random, adding new categories to accommodate strategic priorities that did not fit into the initial topic classes, and in the end, there were 43 topics (including an "other" category for nine strategic priorities that could not be otherwise classified).[7]

Our discussion of simplifying strategy is drawn from an action research project done in conjunction with the Young Presidents' Organization (YPO), a global network of young chief executives, headquartered in Irving, Texas. Between 2011 and 2014, four cohorts of 10 member companies from the YPO participated in a program to help them translate their broad vision or mission into a strategy and concrete priorities, and then develop simple rules to ensure these guidelines shaped important activities and decisions within their company. The CEO and top team of each company went through a structured process to articulate their strategy and convert it into a set of midterm priorities to guide execution.[8]

The survey data cited in the article is from a survey designed to measure an organization's ability to execute its strategy, developed by Donald Sull and Rebecca Homkes. Between 2012 and 2017, the survey was administered to 11,017 managers in 423 organizations. The online survey consists of 69 questions designed to assess how well strategic priorities are understood throughout the organization, the strength of corporate values and norms, and how well management practices such as resource allocation and incentives support strategy execution.

What companies call their corporate objectives doesn't matter; S&P 500 companies use a variety of labels, ranging from the mundane (strategic priorities, areas of focus, strategic objectives) to the exotic (Microsoft Corp. referred to "interconnected ambitions" and department store chain Kohl's Corp., headquartered in Menomonee Falls, Wisconsin, talked about "greatness agenda pillars").

Whatever terminology companies use, their objectives share a few characteristics. They typically extend three to five

Common Names for Strategic Priorities Among S&P 500 Companies
S&P 500 companies used a variety of terms to describe the handful of key actions designed to implement their strategy.

years—shorter than that is too tactical, longer too visionary. They are limited to a handful—of S&P 500 companies publicizing their objectives, 78% listed a total of three to five. And they are strategic in the sense that they describe specific actions that will help the company execute its strategy, as opposed to achieving financial targets or acting on corporate values.

Many executives tell us that they use strategic priorities but report that the approach isn't working as well as they had hoped. To set the strategic agenda and drive implementation effectively, we have found that strategic priorities need to balance guidance with flexibility, counterbalance the inertia of business as usual, and unify disparate parts of the business. Crafting strategic priorities that do all of these things—and do them well—is a tall order. The remainder of this article will describe the seven

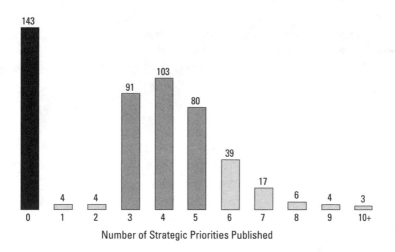

Number of Strategic Priorities Published

Strategic Priorities Among S&P 500 Companies
Among S&P 500 companies, 71% published strategic priorities, and most listed between three and five priorities.

Characteristics of effective strategic priorities

✓ Limit objectives to a handful	Limiting strategic priorities focuses on what matters most and can serve as a forcing mechanism to drive difficult trade-offs among conflicting objectives.
✓ Focus on the midterm	Strategic priorities typically require three to five years to accomplish. Annual goals are too tactical, and longer-term goals too abstract to provide concrete guidance.
✓ Pull toward the future	Strategic priorities should focus on initiatives that position the company to succeed in the future, not reinforce business models or strategies that worked in the past.
✓ Make the hard calls	Strategy is about choice, and strategic priorities should tackle head-on the most consequential and difficult trade-offs facing the company.
✓ Address critical vulnerabilities	Strategic priorities should address the elements of the strategy that are most important for success and most likely to fail in execution.
✓ Provide concrete guidance	Guidance should be concrete enough that leaders throughout the organization could use the strategic priorities to decide what to focus on, what not to do, and what to stop doing. Metrics matter.
✓ Align the top team	Strategic priorities should provide a framework for how the company as a whole will succeed. To do so, they must be agreed upon by all members of the top leadership team.

Strategic Priorities Among S&P 500 Companies

This checklist can help managers assess whether their strategic priorities will be effective in setting a shared strategic agenda for their organization and driving implementation of that agenda.

characteristics of effective strategic priorities, explain why they matter, and suggest practical diagnostics managers can use to assess their company's strategic priorities.

Limit the Number of Priorities to a Handful

Restricting the number of strategic priorities to three to five has several advantages. Most obviously, a small number of them will be easier to understand, communicate throughout the organization, and remember.[9] Rather than overwhelming employees with the full set of all choices and interdependencies that make up a company's strategy, communicating a few strategic priorities can focus attention, effort, and resources on the things that matter most now. The best priorities serve as strategic guardrails. If they know the parameters they must work within, managers and employees can fill in the blanks based on their local knowledge and circumstances.

Having too many priorities is a mistake, but having too few can be a problem as well. One wholesale energy company we studied declared a single strategic priority: "to manage risk and preserve value." This was a worthy goal to be sure, but one that was far too abstract to provide useful guidance to employees. A single priority in isolation is rarely enough to drive a strategy that requires multiple initiatives to work together.

Focus on Midterm Objectives
Strategic priorities act as a bridge between long-term aspirations—embodied in a vision or mission—and annual or quarterly objectives. The types of initiatives that have the biggest impact (for example, building data analytics capabilities, integrating online and physical stores, or entering a new market) typically take a few years. Of course, there are exceptions: A financial turnaround, for example, would require an immediate focus on short-term cash generation and debt reduction. But in general, we've found a good rule of thumb is "three to five in three to five"—three to five strategic priorities that can be accomplished in three to five years.

Once you've set midterm priorities, it's important to stick to them. When a team announces five-year priorities and changes them a year later, employees dismiss those objectives (and their successors) as the "flavor of the month" that they can safely ignore. British fashion retailer Burberry Group plc offers a good example of staying the course.[10] When Angela Ahrendts joined Burberry as CEO in 2006, she announced five strategic priorities (including intensifying nonapparel sales, accelerating retail-led growth, and investing in underpenetrated markets) and selected quantitative metrics for each. Ahrendts stuck with the priorities for seven years until she left the company, updating employees and investors regularly on progress toward each goal, which reinforced the message and the company's commitment to achieving those objectives. During this period, Burberry's share price handily outperformed competitors' and the broader market.

Pull Toward the Future

Strategy should guide how a company will create and capture value going forward, rather than codifying how it made money in the past. In dynamic markets, ongoing success typically requires innovation and change. The things that position a company for the future—for example, entering unfamiliar markets, building innovative business models, or developing new capabilities—differ from business as usual. Both are critical, but they often pull in opposite directions.

Maintaining a healthy balance between the status quo and innovation is hard work. Well-oiled capabilities, established resources, organizational structure, metrics, and rewards favor a company's legacy business, and employees will naturally default to activities that are familiar and straightforward and produce predictable results.[11] Keeping the trains running in the core business is necessary for success, but these routine activities will usually take care of themselves without having to be prioritized at the corporate level.

Innovation and change, by contrast, require ongoing attention. New activities are difficult, frustrating, and uncertain,

and they require sustained effort and monitoring to be successful. This is where strategic prioritization can help. Prioritizing
forward-looking initiatives can tip the scales in favor of the
activities that can ensure future vitality but are most likely to fail
without sustained effort.

Striking the right balance between sustaining a legacy business and building for the future requires judgment—there is
no cookie-cutter template for getting it right. To gauge whether
things are in balance, we suggest leaders look at the mix of priorities in terms of those that support and refine the current
business model (for example, cost reduction, operational excellence, serving current customers, extending existing products)
versus the objectives that take the company in a new direction
(for example, entering new markets, building digital capability,
undertaking nonincremental innovation). Leaders can also ask
how different the business would look in three to five years if
they were to achieve all their objectives. No mix of priorities
is right for every company, but we have found that leadership
teams that don't examine their strategic priorities tend to over-
value business as usual.

Make the Hard Calls

Apple Inc. CEO Steve Jobs often stood at a whiteboard during
strategy retreats and personally led discussions among the company's top 100 leaders to set strategic priorities.[12] The assembled
team would generate a long list of possibilities, and after much
wrangling and discussion, they would whittle them down to a
rank-ordered list of 10, at which point Jobs would strike out the
bottom seven to ensure the company focused on the most critical priorities.

In organizations of any size, there will be dozens or hundreds
of competing and often conflicting priorities. The discipline

of whittling down priorities to a handful can force a leadership team to surface, discuss, and ultimately make a call on the most consequential trade-offs the company faces in the next few years. When executives make the hard calls and communicate them through the ranks, they provide clear guidance on the contentious issues likely to arise when executing strategy. But making trade-offs among competing priorities is difficult—they are dubbed "tough calls" for a reason. Prioritizing different objectives results in "winners" and "losers" in terms of visibility, resources, and corporate support. Many leadership teams go to great lengths to avoid conflict and, as a result, end up producing toothless strategic priorities.

A common way to avoid conflict is to designate everything as "strategic"—one S&P 500 company, for example, listed a dozen strategic objectives. Another way leadership teams resist making difficult calls is by combining multiple objectives into a single strategic priority. A large retailer, for example, listed six key business priorities. So far, so good, but when you dug into the so-called priorities—"focus on the fundamentals of the business," for example—the apparent discipline proved illusory. "Focus on the fundamentals" included, among other items, inventory management, cost cutting, customers, product categories, in-store experience, execution, speed, agility, lead-time reductions, and developing and retaining staff. If leaders dodge the hard trade-offs, their priorities provide little useful guidance to the troops.

Leadership teams also avoid prioritization by burying their strategic priorities among competing mandates and guidelines. The CEO of a large European bank (not one of the S&P 500), for example, was pleased when his team agreed on four strategic priorities during their strategy retreat. That was the good news. The bad news was that the team tacked them onto what the bank was already attempting to do, using three transformation initiatives, a four-part declaration of principles, four customer service priorities, five core beliefs, eight rules of conduct, nine corporate values, 20 promises to stakeholders, and 120 key performance indicators. Baffled employees ignored the latest directive and carried on with what they were already doing.

Address Critical Vulnerabilities

Even when you recognize the importance of making the hard calls, it's often difficult to know where to focus. Strategy is inherently complex, and the sheer number of possible objectives can overwhelm teams. So how can executives move from a complex strategy to a handful of strategic priorities?

A key insight comes from military strategists, who have long acknowledged the complexity of armed conflict.[13] Military planners often visualize the field of operations as a complex system of enemies, allies, infrastructure, popular support, and other features that collectively influence who wins and who loses a war. They then hone in on the so-called "centers of gravity"—the parts of the system that are both critical to the enemy's success and most vulnerable to attack.[14]

Business leaders can deploy a similar approach by identifying "critical vulnerabilities"—the elements of their own strategy that are most important for success and most likely to fail in execution. In for-profit organizations, pinpointing the most important actions means thinking through—and, ideally, quantifying—how the objective would help create and capture economic value. How much would a potential priority increase customers' willingness to pay? How much would it decrease costs to serve target customers? How much would a priority deter new entrants or competitors by building a moat around the fortress? What new revenue streams would a proposed objective open up?

Some elements of a company's strategy—for example, a well-known brand or well-honed capabilities—will be critical to success but may not require sustained attention or investment. While important, these may not be priorities. Instead, companies should prioritize initiatives or activities that are at the greatest risk of failure without the sustained focus and investment support that strategic priorities can provide. When identifying critical vulnerabilities, it's important to look at both the elements of strategy that are at risk due to external factors (such as shifting customer preferences, disruptive technologies, or new entrants) and internal challenges (need for culture change, organizational complexity, or need to build new competencies).

Provide Concrete Guidance

A company's strategic objectives should be tangible enough that leaders and employees throughout the organization can use them to prioritize their activities and investments (and also to help them decide what to stop doing). Unfortunately, many leadership teams agree on vague abstractions that everyone can get on board with, confident that the resulting platitudes will not constrain their options. American Airlines Group Inc., for example, listed strategic imperatives including "focus on our customers' needs and wants," "be an industry leader," and "look to the future." Clearly, a company's strategic priorities are too vague when you can't guess the company (or even the industry) by reading them.

Many associate concrete guidance with financial targets. Revenue and profitability goals are indeed specific, but they

American Airlines *Five Imperatives*	**Southwest Airlines** *Strategic Initiatives*
❶ Focus on customers' needs and wants.	❶ Integration of Southwest's and AirTran's network and operations
❷ Be an industry leader.	❷ Fleet modernization
❸ Engage our team members.	❸ Continued incorporation of the larger Boeing 737-800 aircraft into the Southwest fleet
❹ Provide a return for our investors.	
❺ Look to the future.	❹ International capabilities and new reservation system
	❺ Continued growth of Southwest's Rapid Rewards frequent flyer program

Vague versus Concrete Strategic Priorities

Strategic priorities must provide concrete guidance to the troops. American Airlines' Five Imperatives for 2014 were so vague that they could have applied to any industry. By contrast, Southwest Airlines' Strategic Initiatives were concrete enough to guide action and investments.

quantify where management wants to end up without providing direction on how the company should get there. Using financial targets as strategic priorities, then, is the business equivalent of a coach telling the team what the final score should be without explaining how to beat their opponents.

Rather than relying solely on financial targets, leaders should start with the key actions required to execute their strategy, and translate these into metrics that provide concrete guidance on what success would look like. By tracking progress against metrics, leaders can maintain a sense of urgency over the months or years required to achieve the goal, identify what's not working to make midcourse corrections, and communicate progress along the way—even before financial results are in—to keep key stakeholders on board.

Top executives can quickly assess whether their strategic priorities are sufficiently concrete by asking middle managers what they would stop doing based on the priorities. The answers will quickly expose fuzzy objectives. Leaders can also test concreteness by taking each strategic priority, stripping it of flowery prose and buzzwords, and seeing what's left. For example, once you remove the marketing spin and buzzwords from a statement like "We put muscle behind innovation, making a step change in the pace of commercialization," there's not much substance left.

Align the Top Team

Unfortunately, lack of agreement on company objectives is fairly common among top teams. As part of our research on strategy execution, we surveyed more than 10,000 managers across more than 400 organizations. When asked how closely members of their company's top executive team agreed on key priorities, nearly one-third said senior executives focused on their own agendas or that there were clear factions within the top team.[15]

The reality is actually worse than the survey results suggest. In addition to asking senior executives if they agree on the company's priorities, we asked them to list their company's key priorities over the next few years. In the typical company, barely half of the executives voiced the same company-wide priorities.[16] Indeed, in terms of shared strategic priorities, we found that two-thirds of the top executives were on the same page in just 27% of the companies we studied—hardly a recipe for successful execution among the rest.

Executing strategy often requires different parts of the company to work together in new ways (such as when a company moves from selling stand-alone products to integrated solutions, or when a retailer blends online and in-store sales). Strategic

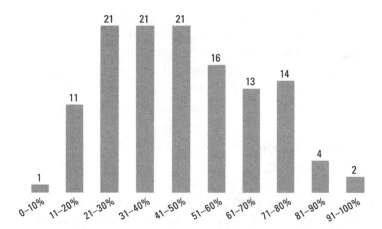

Sample of 124 companies at which four or more top team members listed strategic priorities. Histogram of companies by percentage of top executives who can list three of their company's top five strategic priorities. Companies have a median of 4,843 and a mean of 33,390 employees.

Most Top Teams Disagree on Priorities

We asked the top teams of 124 companies to list their key priorities over the next few years and then analyzed the overlap in their responses. The ranges at the bottom of the chart indicate the amount of overlap in executives' agreement on top priorities. The figures above the bars indicate the number of companies that fell into each range.

priorities should reinforce one another to ensure the different parts of the company are moving in tandem. At a minimum, the priorities shouldn't conflict with one another or pull the organization in opposing directions. The best strategic priorities hang together and tell a coherent story about how the company as a whole will create value in the future. They should also provide guidance on how to adjudicate the conflicts that will inevitably arise as different parts of the organization try to execute the strategy in the trenches.

Strategic priorities should lay out what matters for the company as a whole to win and reflect the interdependencies among the choices. If senior executives pursue goals that aren't aligned with one another, the disagreements will filter down the silos, and the various teams will work at cross-purposes.

Management teams sometimes diverge because each function wants to promote its own pet objective. Human resources might want to say something about "world-class talent," for example, while finance might want to highlight how the company delivers "industry-leading shareholder returns." Rarely is anyone considering the trade-offs among these objectives, their interdependencies, or whether meeting unit-level objectives will affect the company's ability to succeed. These priorities can reinforce, rather than break down, organizational silos.

Executives rightly focus on how to craft a great strategy but often pay less attention to how their strategy can be implemented throughout a complex organization. To steer activity in the right direction, a strategy should be translated into a few guardrails that provide basic guidance while leaving scope for adaptation as circumstances change. Strategic priorities are a common tool to drive execution, but in many cases, these objectives are not as effective as they could be. By following a few guidelines, executives can articulate a strategy that can be communicated, understood, and executed.

4

Leading in a Time of Increased Expectations

Lynn J. Good, interviewed by Paul Michelman

When you lead one of the world's largest electric utilities, you deal with a rather interesting set of challenges. For example:

- A large percentage of your workforce is nearing retirement, yet your industry does not seem to hold the attractiveness of the dynamic technology companies you must compete with for young talent.

- You manage stakeholders who often have opposing interests, which means whatever you do to satisfy one risks alienating another.

- After decades of stability and uniformity, your customers' expectations for service, choice, and customization have dramatically transformed and diverged.

- Your industry is exposed to changes in public policies that are under continual debate—at the local, national, and global levels.

- And while nature is literally the source of your power, it can also be your most vicious enemy, especially when huge swaths of your customers live in hurricane zones like the Carolinas and Florida.

Meet Lynn J. Good, chairman, president, and CEO of Charlotte, North Carolina-based Duke Energy Corp. Good, whose calm and upbeat demeanor belies the very long set of complex tensions she faces every day, met with *MIT Sloan Management Review* editor in chief Paul Michelman at Duke's headquarters in Charlotte, with further exchanges via email. What follows is a condensed and edited version of their conversation about leadership, strategy, and an industry undergoing dramatic transformation.

MIT Sloan Management Review: The first topic I'd like to cover is industry transformation and the nature of competition. You wrote recently that the transformational change the electric industry is undergoing "is surprisingly intense." What are the key drivers of this surprisingly intense transformation?

Lynn J. Good: I point to three things: customer expectations, technology, and public policy. What's surprising is that all three of them are changing at the same time. To have rapid advancement on three distinct dimensions simultaneously makes for an extraordinary transformation.

Let's look at how our customer relationships have evolved. And to do that, we have to look at where our industry has come from. We are engineers who built big networks. We manage assets. We maintain the reliability of those assets. Our traditional focus was on the network, not the customer. And then you have today's world of empowered consumers, who expect choice, convenience at their fingertips, and to have their questions answered in real time. Historically, we have not invested in the ways necessary to keep pace with their expectations.

Now that's changing. The amount of capital that we're deploying around new solutions for customers is more than it was

We have to keep
up with what
customers expect
from an experience:
information, control,
convenience,
and choice.

five years ago—and a lot more than it was 10 or 15 years ago. We have to keep up with what customers expect from an experience: information, control, convenience, and choice. People expect that from their energy provider just as they do with all the other services in their lives.

What are some of those investments? What are some of the dynamics of the new relationship?

First, there's mobile. Customers today care deeply about where their power comes from. They may want a fully green solution. They expect choice about how to pay their bill. They want access to data on their usage. People are accustomed to having unique customer-specific information about the products that they're buying. Mobile apps are the centerpiece of giving customers access to the data and options they are seeking.

And then we are putting new devices on our systems: smart meters, sensing devices, and communication technologies that allow the network to gather and deliver all this information.

And we need to address our legacy IT [information technology] systems. Our legacy customer system was pegged to a meter. It didn't know if you had a telephone number. We didn't have your email address. We knew the customer as simply a meter. Well, that doesn't work anymore. Those legacy systems weren't built for the customer expectations and functionality we've been discussing. We need to invest to bring them up to date.

Given the complexity of your industry relative to the other industries that consumers interact with, how reasonable or unreasonable are customer expectations?

Well, I'm not sure it matters, because there's no customer who thinks they're unreasonable. They have expectations, and it's my job to meet them. If someone has an expectation that the delivery or service window should be two hours and we're telling them eight hours, which means they have to take a day off of work, we need to adjust that.

Here's another example. We bill you when we read your meter. We run a big network, and we tend to do things on our own timeline. Now, think about a senior citizen who has a monthly check that comes the first week of the month. They want very much for their electric bill to come the first week of the month, too. It helps them manage their life. Why can't we send the bill the first week of the month? Or why can't we provide an option where they can send us a prepayment on the first of the month? It's a reasonable expectation and something that other industries accommodate for customers all the time.

We're not solving rocket science problems here. No one is asking me to explain how the nuclear reactor works. What people want is to be able to pay their bill when they want. They want to know how much energy they're using. They want to know how it compares to last year. They want to know if they're about to go over their budget. Those are things that we should be able to enable, but it takes investment.

Presumably, customer expectations are a moving target, particularly now, with new smartphones coming out every year with new abilities, right? How do you think about keeping pace?

It's a really important question for us. Think about the big legacy systems we operate. Historically, we have worked with long development windows. Define requirements, design it, test it, and roll it out. It might take five years. Now, we are shifting toward agile methodologies, so we're delivering customer solutions much more quickly. We're testing, piloting, getting feedback, and continuing to move forward. We can't live with a five-year cycle.

That's not to say that we're necessarily going fast enough, but we're trying to keep pace with what we know to be a rapidly developing set of expectations.

There's a cultural element to this. We are trying to foster an environment where flexibility, change, and agility is the way we do business. And this is where you start to see some of the tensions with the complexity of our business. We have safety and reliability to be concerned with; we manage big equipment. It takes us a long time to do things at times. But nonetheless, we have to be an organization that embraces change and is agile enough to keep moving.

I see that agility at two levels. It's not only products and services and trying to keep pace with customers, but it's increasing the metabolism of the organization to embrace change internally more readily.

As the organization's top leader, how do you talk about this?

Over the last year, I have been working to define for the organization what I call our leadership imperative. I'm trying to paint a picture of what it means to lead at Duke Energy.

There are five elements of the imperative. The first one is "live our purpose," which is nothing more than a way to say that we have a very important mission. People count on us 24 hours a day, seven days a week, all seasons, all times. I'm looking for personal conviction and commitment. I won't get the discretionary effort I need—think about our Hurricane Irma response—if our leaders don't feel a clear connection between their purpose as a leader and the big mission of Duke Energy.

The second is that you must be a leader who understands how to lead change. You can set a vision and you can lead your organization toward the vision in an agile, flexible way. You embrace all of the things we are talking about here that are transforming in the business.

The third is to deliver results the right way. We can sit in this conference room and talk about all kinds of good things, but we need to deliver an outcome to our customers, an outcome to our stakeholders. And it has to be the right way—with safety, integrity, and customer service.

The fourth, "work as one," is our term for how we go about working together in this big, siloed organization with our nuclear professionals and distribution employees and legal experts and regulatory managers. The outside world doesn't see us that way. They want one solution from Duke Energy. If you are a leader wrestling with a problem that requires you to go across the company, the company needs to support you. We need to show up as Duke Energy, not as leaders of siloed organizations. That requires great collaboration, joint problem solving, and enterprise leadership.

And finally, "inspire our employees." We can't be successful in any period of change or transformation unless we have absolutely every employee aligned and getting up in the morning with enthusiasm about how they're going to add to the future of the organization. This part of the imperative means embracing inclusion—embracing different cultures and generations, from millennials to people who are nearing the end of their career. It's leading across geographies. The focus on inspiration emphasizes that we win as an organization when all 29,000 of us are moving in the same direction.

We need to show up as Duke Energy, not as leaders of siloed organizations. That requires great collaboration, joint problem solving, and enterprise leadership.

I talk a lot about these leadership imperatives. We're developing leaders with these qualities in mind. We talk about leaders as being strong in one quality and not as strong in others. We look at what competencies underlie the imperatives. How do we put those into a leadership academy for developing leaders? They are a part of ongoing performance discussions so that we are translating the ideal of what we want into actual applications in the ways we behave.

It sounds like you are emphasizing behavior and activities that may be hard to quantify and measure.

There are plenty of things to quantify around here. We are flush with metrics. Whether it's earnings or reliability or capacity or generation or turnover rates, we're a metric-rich environment. We're accustomed to running the business by metrics. But I don't think running the business by metrics alone gets you through a period of transformation.

Has your approach to planning evolved?

Over the past five years, I've probably spent more time on planning than in the previous 10 years combined.

We are dealing with so many more variables today. We've talked about a number of them already. Then there is the focus on renewables and curtailing our reliance on fossil fuels; deregulation; and changes in market structure. These changes can incent lots of different, even conflicting, behaviors and decisions.

So we undertake an ongoing assessment of all of these trends to develop the Duke point of view. And then we plan scenarios in which we are wrong. What happens if there is no more shale gas or there is a regulatory mandate to go 100% in a new direction? Amidst the scenarios, we need to identify where we believe—under the majority of the circumstances—it's going to make sense to invest.

You can have a horizon probably through 2020, maybe 2025, on that basis. I think renewables that are cost-effective are a good investment. Investing in our grid makes sense—to accommodate renewables, develop more storm-resistant infrastructure, and address all these customer expectations we've talked about. Cybersecurity is another.

And we believe natural gas is a good place to invest, at least in the medium term, since we don't have a set of technology solutions that will make reliance on 100% renewable energy possible. Meanwhile, I know coal is under pressure. I know nuclear is challenged. What else do I have in my portfolio of choices that complements the renewable, lower-carbon solutions and that I believe could allow me to keep delivering reliable 24/7 power?

We're constantly testing our assumptions. We have signposts that we monitor—prices, adoption rates, regulatory trends, public policy, what's happening in the [US Department of Energy's] National Labs. What's happening in Europe, Australia, and other markets that may be ahead of us on some of these issues? We are challenging our view of the future.

How frequently do you revisit your assumptions and objectives?

Very frequently. In our business, as in many, you're always challenged on both the short and long term. How much time do I spend on quarterly earnings versus the longer horizon?

We are trying to manage that through process. First, my weekly leadership staff meeting focuses on current events: What's coming at us right now; where are we on the current year plan? And then, every couple of months, we take a day to a day and a half to look out further. We revisit renewables and what's going on with battery technology. We'll bring in an outside speaker—for example, someone who has embraced agile techniques. And then we bring those topics in at the board level, so that every board meeting has a longer-term topic.

We take a similar approach to strategy. We set up a framework that articulates what we believe are foundational elements to success in this dynamic industry. I'll give you several examples: meeting customer expectations, being very good at stakeholder engagement, and operating with excellence—which we absolutely must do. We have to deliver safe, reliable, environmentally responsible power, day in and day out. If we don't do those things well, it really doesn't matter what we're investing in.

Let's talk about people. As your workforce ages, how do you recruit young talent to a very mature industry that might not match their idealism?

I actually do think our industry taps into that idealism, because we do something that matters. Help us figure out how we're going to embrace a 100% renewable future. Come help an industry that matters so much to survive for another 100 years. It will take your creativity and agility to do that.

Energy is a part of the conversation everywhere, so we have a good story to tell young people. And we put them to work with the skills they bring; they are technology-literate, interested in sustainability and innovation, and willing to embrace change. When we complement that with experience, support, and intensive knowledge transfer from our more senior employees, you've got a combination that can work.

Given the earlier part of our conversation about customers' expectations being driven by their experiences with other services or products in their lives, has that led you to think more broadly about where employees come from?

We recently named a chief customer officer from outside the industry, someone who has a background with Disney and United Airlines, to help create the picture for what customer relationships should look like.

In our customer organization, we already have more segmentation experts, more data analytics professionals, more service-oriented people who understand how we can make a better connection with the customers. We'll continue to look at new initiatives through that lens, and I think that will lead to more differentiated hiring over time.

How do you think about finding the right balance between generating cleaner energy and meeting other demands like affordability?

We sit at an intersection of affordability, reliability, clean, safe. We can't afford to run down any single path all by itself. We can't just say we're going to produce the cheapest power no matter where it comes from. Or that we're going to spend all the money in the world to make sure your power never goes out. Or that we're going to drive carbon emissions down to zero in the next four years. It's impossible to do. No one has the resources to accomplish that. So we are constantly trying to strike the balance. We have targets and expectations around each.

Affordability is really important, whether you are a consumer with low discretionary income or you're an industrial company that's competing against Georgia or China or Latin America.

If you're in heavy manufacturing, the cost of power is one of the top three factors that makes you competitive. We can't walk away from affordability.

We can't walk away from sustainability, either. We need to demonstrate that we are reducing our carbon footprint, that we're being good stewards of water, we're being good stewards of solid waste and recycling, and doing all of the things our customers expect, and frankly, I expect. The communities we operate in expect us to be responsible.

Our carbon emissions are down 30% from 2005. We're working toward 40%. It's going to take a combination of renewables, natural gas conversion, and energy efficiency for us to continue to move in that direction. Some stakeholders may argue we're not moving fast enough. Others may argue that we are prioritizing sustainability over lower prices.

And that's just one part of the business. We are always trying to work with stakeholders to find common ground—to manage the tensions between different priorities and to keep the business running, affordable, safe, reliable, clean.

I'd like to hear your thoughts on where we are with the number of women leading large organizations.

I believe great progress has been made. Now, great against a low base, right? But if you look at our industry in particular, there are more women CEOs than certainly when I started in the industry. I look at the executive ranks here at Duke. Our general counsel is a woman, my head of administration is a woman. We have very important leaders at the next level who are women.

The question is generally, is it enough? Is it fast enough? Are we on a curve that's going to lead to percentages that are more consistent with percentages entering the workforce? When do we get to 50/50? When do we get to 30%? I think that's the challenge for diversity in general. How do you continue to recruit, promote, develop, and mentor an increasingly diverse population?

And I think the business imperative for this is undeniable. We absolutely must do it. The way we think about it at Duke is that it's a pipeline issue first. We need to make sure that we see enough diverse candidates in our hiring practices. And that we have intentional development programs and mentoring programs directed at helping people be successful.

Are there other levers that we can be pulling?

I wish I knew what the other ways were. I don't think there's a single solution to this. To get to the C-suite, you need to put together 25 to 30 years of career. There are a lot of things that could happen in 25 or 30 years. The objective is to get a lot of diverse talent in the pipeline so you're building a robust set of candidates with that type of experience.

When it comes to recruiting, we've been trying to cast broader nets. We've done more sourcing—where we go find people, as opposed to waiting for them to come to us. We've tried recruitment boot camps for our field crews in diverse communities to try to increase the interest and understanding of what our job opportunities are. There's a lot of work to do to continue that pipeline development.

And what about board representation?

I think it's a similar issue. There's been some discussion by certain institutional investors of trying to get to 30% board representation for women.

Board recruitment is challenging. You want diversity, but you don't want people who are "overboarded." You should sit on

Think about the complex world we've been discussing. Wouldn't you love to have different points of view on how we deal with these really tough business issues?

one or two boards; three, maybe, if you're retired. There's a lot of demand for director candidates who will increase the diversity in a boardroom, so there's a pipeline issue there, too. If we can get more diversity in the C-suites of corporations, the diversity of the boards will improve as well.

I'm a believer that diverse perspectives are very valuable. You think about the complex world we've been discussing. Wouldn't you love to have different points of view on how we deal with these really tough business issues? Diversity is a business imperative, just like good capital stewardship.

II

Evolve

5

Don't Get Caught in the Middle

Paul Michelman

Sometimes things move so fast in our digitized world that it can feel as if there is no safe place to position yourself—or your organization. How do you anticipate where to go next—whether considering your company's strategy or your own career—when the winds of change sweep from every direction? You simply can't know the right move for certain. And even when you do make a good call, the clock is ticking; you'll soon face a new threat of obsolescence. As I've written in the past, we all need to accept that change is continual; we must learn to embrace change rather than fight it. Similarly, we need to accept that there are no safe havens—for us or our companies. We simply must be prepared to stay on the move.

But whatever you do next, wherever you go, don't head for the middle. Not the middle of a relationship, not the middle of an organization. It's a bad time to be an intermediary—at least in the traditional sense of the word.

As the makers of products seek to close the distance to those who buy and use those products, and as layers of traditional management hierarchy fall away, the real worth is increasingly found at the extremes of value chains and organizations, rather than at the center.

There was once a time when the "middleman" was an indispensable resource. Intermediaries facilitated transactions between producers and consumers; they interpreted high-level corporate strategy and connected it to frontline execution; they monitored and herded; and they closed the gaps between disconnected entities that required one another for survival.

But one by one, they are being replaced—if not rendered obsolete—by technology.

- Digital platforms are convening direct connections between traditionally intermediated sides of markets by the thousands—in retailing, dating, personal transportation, entertainment, product development, and so on.

- Within organizations, advanced communication technologies—from corporate messaging apps today to facial recognition and emotion-sensing technologies tomorrow—combined with distributed leadership models are slowly but surely threatening traditional middle-management functions.

- New industrial technologies like additive manufacturing will eliminate links throughout legacy supply chains. For example, a company that can make a needed replacement part through 3-D printing doesn't need to purchase that part from a distributor.

- We are only now just scratching the surface of the internet of things (IoT). IoT promises to deepen connections between manufacturers and end users of their products—and that threatens many traditional intermediaries.

- And if I were in a field such as financial services, I would already be looking at blockchain with a great deal of trepidation.

Who needs the "trusted intermediary" when trust has already been confirmed through blockchain technology?

For most of the industrial age, we took the value of intermediaries as a given. Organizational models were built on the assumption of their value. But the more we encounter example after example of their redundancy, the more we will see middlemen as usurpers of value rather than creators.

Most intermediaries will not disappear overnight. For instance, there are few organizational models that can withstand the wholesale removal of entire management layers in one fell swoop. But over the long term, genus *Go-betweenus* may well find itself on the endangered list.

The intermediaries that persevere will be those that adapt. They will produce unique value, adding something to a transaction or relationship that is—at least for a time—irreplaceable. They will provide a bridge or translation between two parties who would otherwise be unable to fully appreciate each other. Intermediaries will increasingly become specialists offering customized services that are too expensive or rare for the parties they serve to justify building on their own.

But for the rest, for those middle players who exist by tradition rather than by irreplaceability, the future will not be kind.

6

The Best Response to Digital Disruption

Jacques Bughin and Nicolas van Zeebroeck

The imperative of digital transformation is an insistent buzz in the ears of managers in many industries, even the most unexpected.

Consider the business of funeral homes. Few industries are more sensitive, more personal, and more in need of a human touch than the business of arranging funeral services for a loved one. But a study of funeral providers in Berlin, Germany, describes what happened when impersonal yet less expensive options crept up on this market.[1] Aggressive digital entrants unleashed an unprecedented wave of competition in the late 1990s. Discount online providers used search engine optimization to build dominant market positions, leaving incumbents with little choice but to respond by going online themselves to compete against both digital entrants and each other on pricing—rather than on reputation and relationships.

Few executives would dispute that digitization's disruptive influence is growing—and growing rapidly. But surprisingly little empirical evidence has captured either the magnitude of digital disruption or how incumbents are reacting on a broad scale. Leaders know they have a problem—and know they must react to that problem—but they have little guidance to determine the right course of action.

In a bid to help address the gap, McKinsey & Co. undertook a global survey of C-suite executives to capture how digitization unfolds across industries and how incumbents are responding. With some notable and important exceptions, the answer is: "Not well."

About the Research

McKinsey & Co. recently launched a major survey of C-suite executives on the topic of digitization. The survey captured responses from 2,000 traditional companies in more than 60 countries, from an original panel of more than 15,000 companies. The panel is maintained externally for McKinsey by London-based research company Kantar TNS. It is confidential, with an easy opt-out option to ensure the quality of responses. Survey questions covered companies' growth in revenue and earnings before interest and taxes (EBIT); return on investment from digital initiatives; share of revenue linked to digitization and digital capabilities captured in absolute terms and versus the competition; executives' perceptions of digital disruption; the focus of digital strategy; the scale of digital investment; digital capabilities; the organization of digital strategy; typical organizational challenges; and the degree of management support.[2] This new research leverages this data set to formally analyze the link between the performance of companies, their digital transformation programs, and the dynamics of reaction among companies following digitization. It uses a battery of econometric tests, including fixed effects and instrumental regression techniques, to inform how incumbents should best respond to digitization forces.[3]

The insights that emerged from the survey include the following:

- Across countries, digitization has a significant negative impact on the profits of incumbents through two loop effects: digital entrants competing with incumbents through disruptive models, and incumbents responding to disruption and creating more intense competition with each other.

- These two loop effects suggest that organizations should go on the offensive: A successful digital strategy built on a scale larger than that of the rest of the industry yields the largest returns and may offset the full competitive impact of digitization.

- Our research further suggests companies should consider at least two dimensions when devising the type of bold reactions needed to compete: (1) concentrating on new customer segments rather than exclusively on current customers, and (2) focusing on new ways to resegment the market, instead of relying solely on cost cutting and labor saving through automation.

Few companies are responding appropriately to digital disruption, according to our findings. While 90% of companies indicated that they are engaged in some form of digitization, only 16% said their companies have responded with a bold strategy and at scale. Likewise, only 30% of companies are focusing on new ways to bundle demand or resegment their market. The good news is if your company has yet to fully and adequately engage with digital disruption or has begun going down a path that is not yielding positive results, it's not alone. Thus, leaders in most industries still have a window for putting a bold digital strategy in place. But it may not stay open long.

Two Loops of Disruption

Digitization is a multidimensional concept. It can manifest as automation in the supply chain; a new distribution or customer engagement platform; a virtualized or dematerialized product;

or a strategic shift from product-based to service-based offerings. Taking all these developments into account, our survey indicates that on average 35% of companies' revenues worldwide are digitized.

Full digitization for incumbents on any particular dimension, however, remains exceptional: For instance, only 5% of respondents perceive their product as fundamentally digital, and only 6% reported that all their major business processes are highly digitized.

Given the relatively nascent stages of digitization these figures indicate, some leaders may assume that they have plenty of time to get their digital acts together—or that they can proceed cautiously. That assumption is dangerous. New digital entrants have already seized a significant share of revenue across regions and industries—17% on average, according to our findings, leaving only 83% to the incumbents.

Successful new entrants pose dual threats: They pull industries in new digital directions while gaining a huge head start in reaping the benefits from the new models they are creating. This forces incumbents into a race to catch up. While digital entrants hold 17% of total global revenue, they have 47% of digital revenue. Indeed, in some more digitized sectors, digital entrants already have the upper hand. In the telecommunications sector, entrants command 56% of the digitized portion of the market. In financial services, the split is 50–50.

The First Loop: Digital Entrants Challenge Incumbents

Digitally enabled entrants are creating new competitive dynamics that threaten the bottom lines of incumbents—and doing so with great speed. Consider that 18 months after the introduction of the Google Maps Navigation app for smartphones in 2009, as much as 85% of the market capitalization of the top makers of stand-alone GPS devices had evaporated.[4]

Or consider the banking industry, which faces threats from multiple digital entrants. For example, in China, Alibaba Group Holding Ltd., China's e-commerce giant, became the country's biggest seller of money market funds in just seven months.[5] In October 2016, Facebook Inc. obtained a license from the Central Bank of Ireland that enables the social media company to issue e-money and provide payment services such as credit transfers to customers in all 28 European Union member states.[6] Likewise, Google Inc.'s Gmail service now lets users send money as an email attachment.

Even when the effects are not as profound as in the examples above, the dynamic hurts. Attackers don't simply take market share—they also often put pressure on price, alter customer behavior, and change how value is distributed among industry players.

To estimate the impact of digital entrants, we used multiple econometric equations that linked company growth with digitization and corrected for incumbents' responses. We found that globally, digital disruption is shaving 30% off incumbent revenue growth and 25% off growth in earnings before interest and taxes (EBIT).

While digital entrants boost the size of an industry by increasing latent demand by roughly 0.5% a year, they also aggressively steal share from incumbents via new business models, roughly displacing 2 percentage points of year-on-year growth on average. Further, digital entrants challenge the level of competitiveness in an industry, depleting revenue yield per unit sold by 2% a year. At first glance, the price effect may appear modest, but it directly affects the margins of incumbent companies. With a profit rate of 10%, a 2% drop represents a 20% reduction in profitability.

We find that the more digitally advanced an industry is, the larger the negative impact on incumbents that don't act.[7] In the high-tech sector, for instance, we observed that the negative impact on the revenue-growth trajectory of incumbents that do not respond to digital disruption is four times the average found across sectors. The impact in retail and transport is 50% higher than the average. In contrast, in manufacturing, the effect is only 60% of the average.

Our analysis further suggests that digital disruption hurts slower-growing companies the most. The bottom 25% of companies in terms of growth are experiencing three times greater reduction in annual revenue at the hands of digital disruption than the top quartile.

The Second Loop: Beware the Red Queen

While most executives intuitively understand the pain inflicted on incumbents by digital entrants in the first loop of digitization, the second loop—how legacy companies react to each other—can hurt just as much. In fact, we contend that incumbent responses to digital disruption can trigger "Red Queen" competition[8] in which legacy companies engage in aggressive imitation—first in response to digital entrants and then in response to one another—in a self-reinforcing process. (This kind of competition is named for the Red Queen, a character in Lewis Carroll's *Through the Looking-Glass*, who engages in a foot race in which competitors run hard just to stay in the same place.)

For a prototypical example of Red Queen competition, consider the digital tit-for-tat that has permeated the battle between United Parcel Service Inc. and FedEx Corp. for the overnight package-delivery market. Over the years, when one of the two companies launched a digital innovation such as handheld devices for delivery information, online parcel tracking, or a complete web shipping service, the other added a similar feature not long thereafter. As the competitors responded to moves with countermoves, innovation increasingly gave way to imitation.[9]

Now, think again about how online entrants have forced changes in the way traditional funeral homes market and sell their services. Such changes in competitive behavior are prevalent in many industries. In financial services, for example, as mobile banking made significant inroads and set a new standard and price level for payment services, incumbent banks had to react by reducing or eliminating fees. Following the entry of multiple financial technology startups, Deutsche Bank AG launched an advertising campaign in Belgium comparing banks to supermarkets, asking, "What would happen if your supermarket behaved like your bank does?" The ad shows a cashier charging customers not only for their purchases but also for printing the receipt, for using the conveyor belt, and for not having a loyalty card. The spot concludes: "You wouldn't accept unnecessary charges from your supermarket. Why accept them from your bank? Switch now to Deutschebank.be." When effective changes by the competition put other incumbents in reactive mode, the pressure to follow suit with revenue-reducing moves can be immense.

The automotive industry offers another illustration. As online entrants such as Zipcar, BlaBlaCar, and Uber introduced new business models based on car sharing, auto manufacturers took notice and started investing in similar ventures, considerably expanding the reach and credibility of this emerging part of the market. In 2008, Daimler AG tested a car-sharing service called car2go with its employees in Ulm, Germany. By the end

When effective changes by the competition put other incumbents in reactive mode, the pressure to follow suit with revenue-reducing moves can be immense.

of 2016, the service, now available to the wider public, was operating more than 14,000 vehicles across 30 cities in Europe, the United States, and China. In 2011, BMW Group partnered with Sixt AG to launch a similar service called DriveNow (introduced as ReachNow in the United States in 2016). In October 2016, BMW's digital platform had about 4,000 BMW and Mini vehicles in operation across 12 cities and was already reported to be profitable.[10] In December 2016, Volkswagen Group announced the creation of MOIA, a new Volkswagen company that will develop mobility services. Earlier that year, General Motors Co. launched a similar initiative called Maven, and Paris-based Groupe PSA named its own mobility sharing service Free2Move in 2017. Meanwhile, Ford Motor Co. purchased San Francisco-based shuttle-bus startup Chariot Transit Inc. for a reported price of about $65 million. The proliferation of digital ventures launched by incumbents increases the competitive pressure on emerging mobility models and compromises their profitability. In an attempt to gain economies of scale, Daimler and BMW are said to be investigating the potential merger of their respective initiatives, car2go and DriveNow.[11]

Incumbents need to be careful when they find themselves in Red Queen competition, as the effect is substantial. In our econometric research, we estimated the total effect of digital disruption on company growth trajectories and then assessed the share of the depressive effect attributable to the first and second loops respectively. The results indicated that the two loops contribute more or less equally to the erosion of incumbents' revenue and profit margins. Digital new entrants and Red Queen competitors each shave some 30% off revenue and profit growth of incumbents on average across industries, compared with the picture of a world without digitization.

Bold Responses Required

Our research suggests that the average company has reacted poorly to both loops of digital disruption. Measuring reactions to digitization on two dimensions, we find that the average company has neither sufficiently adapted its corporate strategy to address the new realities of competition nor engaged in a digital transformation at scale.

Two-thirds of the executives in our survey said their companies have not made any fundamental changes to their corporate strategy, while only one in five companies has engaged in a significant transformation of its business portfolio. Moreover, our survey finds that even among companies engaging in a digital strategy, few are doing it in alignment with their broader business and corporate strategies. Only 25% of C-suite executives said their companies have fully integrated their digital and corporate strategies.

We divided company responses to digital disruption into four categories: weak, medium, semibold, and bold. Each company has been assigned to one of these categories according to the intensity of its strategic response (from "no or ad hoc responses" to "changes to the long-term corporate strategy") and level of investments in digital technology relative to its competitors (from "significantly underinvesting" to "significantly overinvesting").

Of the companies in our sample, 22% have made a weak response and 28% a medium response. Thirty-four percent have adopted what we characterize as a semibold response by adopting either a bold strategy or by overinvesting in digital. The remaining 16% of companies surveyed have developed what we label a bold digital strategy at scale.

Our analysis suggests that only a successful response that is both bold and integrated fully can yield revenue and profit trajectories that are higher postdigitization than predigitization.

Taking both the intensity of the response and the degree of integration into account, we find that barely 8% have both responded offensively and integrated their digital strategy fully into the corporate strategy. This is a huge missed opportunity: Our analysis suggests that only a successful response that is both bold and integrated fully can yield revenue and profit trajectories that are higher postdigitization than predigitization.

To understand why requires us to go back to the logic of the two loops. Any reaction to digital pressure is likely to be matched by Red Queen competition of the same magnitude. That means companies need to act more boldly than the average incumbent if they wish to outperform their industry. And the reaction must be more than simply bold: It should be appropriate in the face of digital entrants. Because digital entry is usually disruptive, the incumbent must also be disruptive—and quickly—to both limit the loss of competitive ground against digital newcomers and take advantage of other incumbents that are slow to respond.

We arrived at this conclusion by assessing the impact on revenue from different strategic reactions. In doing so, three clear messages emerged:

- **Incumbent companies are usually better off reacting than not reacting.** Digital initiatives tend to exploit latent demand in an industry, creating a positive market expansion effect. For example, people may spend more time watching videos or listening to music because online delivery is more accessible, or they may be more likely to buy an extra product online because the seller recommends it based on previous purchases. However, this benefit from digital initiatives is compensated for by the depressive effect of the two loops, and, as a result, the net effect of digital reactions tends to be very modest overall.

- **On average, bold, at-scale responses pay off twice as much as semibold reactions and three times as much as medium reactions.** There is some variation by industry, but it is not dramatic. In telecom and high tech, for instance, bold, at-scale reactions have 2.5 times greater payoff than medium reactions. In manufacturing, the payoff is 2.2 times greater, and in retail and media, it is 1.9 times greater. Given that we estimated a medium reaction is worth 1.5 points of EBIT growth a year and about 2 percentage points in revenue growth per year, the effect of a successful bold, at-scale move is roughly 4.5 points in EBIT and 6 points in revenue—the same positive payoff as the original negative impact of digital entry.

- **To do better than just break even on digital disruption, companies must also integrate digital strategy into their corporate strategy.** Companies whose responses met our criteria for being both bold and integrated produced 3 to 4 percentage points more annual revenue growth and the same EBIT growth as before digitization.

Three Opportunities

Our research finds that only a small minority of companies are successfully undertaking a digital transformation consistent with a bold corporate strategy. But among these companies, three clear tactics emerge:

- **Develop new customer segments.** It is a prerequisite for success that companies focus on developing new customer segments rather than just defending existing business lines through cost cutting, automation, or service improvements for existing customers. Medialaan NV, a leading free-to-air video broadcaster in Belgium, spotted the inevitable shift in

video consumption by youngsters to platforms such as Netflix or YouTube. In a bold response, Medialaan bought Mobile
Vikings, a mobile virtual operator with attractive data plans.
The strategy: Transform itself into the leading online social
video platform for Flemish teenagers. Medialaan not only has
diversified its revenue base to include data plans but also has
been able to reengage with a lost segment—the teens—and
now advertises its television programs to them more effectively. It is one of the few traditional broadcast companies to
grow its TV audience in the youth segment.

- **Introduce new business models.** Innovative companies are
  experimenting with business models intended to disrupt their
  own legacy strategies. Around the turn of the century, Schibsted Media Group, headquartered in Oslo, Norway, observed
  something that most media companies saw in their newspa-
  per businesses: Print classified advertising was beginning to
  dry up. Rather than sit idly by and witness the erosion of one
  of its most important revenue streams, Schibsted pulled the
  rug right out from under its own feet by moving its entire
  classified business to a free online marketplace. Today, more
  than 80% of the group's earnings come from commissions on
  sales from its consumer e-commerce platform.[12]

- **Redefine the value chain.** When digital entrants started threatening its payment services business, Commonwealth Bank of
  Australia (CBA) chose to face the disrupters head-on. Instead
  of focusing exclusively on payment services, it developed Pi,
  an open payments platform that hosts an ecosystem of applications and devices for merchants. The platform is open to
  third-party developers, and the bank developed for itself an
  Android-based point-of-sales terminal called Albert, which
  is fully integrated with the Pi payments platform. Equipped

with a card reader and an integrated printer, Albert can be extended with dedicated apps, enabling it to do much more than process payments. Among the first adopters was Earthling Investments Pty. Ltd. of North Adelaide, South Australia, owner of wholesale fuel distributor Mogas Regional Pty. Ltd., also based in North Adelaide. The company is using Albert at its fuel stations to process customer transactions, manage their payments, and receive sales data faster.[13] Although the platform and its ecosystem contribute to the disruption of the traditional banking value-add chain, it also positions CBA to compete with digital entrants. Similarly, while the mortgage side of the banking business is being disrupted by online search and home-financing platforms, CBA updated its digital value chain through an augmented-reality app that gives customers the ability to read a property's sales history and community information by pointing their iPhone camera at the location. When they have found a property that they wish to buy, users can then file a loan application directly in the app, thus positioning CBA strongly against digital and incumbent competitors alike.

Digital disruption is unavoidable, and companies need to react. Those that do not—or that do so in a half-hearted way—are likely to take a major hit on revenue and profits. Those that respond boldly, at scale, and in a way that is fully embedded in their corporate strategy will be positioned to steal revenue and profits from the laggards and emerge from disruption with higher trajectories in both areas.

7

Why Your Company Needs More Collaboration

David Kiron

What distinguishes companies that have built advanced digital capabilities? The ability to collaborate. *MIT Sloan Management Review*'s research finds that a focus on collaboration—both within organizations and with external partners and stakeholders—is central to how digitally advanced companies create business value and establish competitive advantage. These companies recognize that digital transformation blurs—and sometimes obliterates—traditional organizational boundaries and demands a focus on cooperation and collaboration that is unprecedented for most enterprises.

The broad implications of this finding are evident in three separate research projects that *MIT SMR* conducted from 2015 to 2017: a recent survey-based research report on digital business trends, "Achieving Digital Maturity," produced in partnership with Deloitte Digital; a separate survey-based research project focused on the internet of things (IoT); and a case study project exploring data-driven organizations.

While the benefits of collaboration are clear, so too is the reality that many organizations still have a long way to go in making collaboration the priority it needs to be. Less than half of the respondents to our 2016 digital business survey agreed or strongly agreed that "our organization is increasingly organized around cross-functional project teams, not necessarily functions and divisions, to implement digital business priorities."

More Cross-Functional Collaboration

Based on a global survey of more than 3,500 managers and executives, *MIT Sloan Management Review* and Deloitte's third annual report on digital business found that the most digitally advanced companies—those successfully deploying digital technologies and capabilities to improve processes, engage talent across the organization, and drive new value-generating business models— are far more likely to perform cross-functional collaboration. More than 70% of these businesses use cross-functional teams to organize work and charge them with implementing digital business priorities. This compares to less than 30% for organizations in an early stage of digitization.

Digitally advanced organizations recognize and reward collaboration and cross-functional teams—nearly 77% of digitally advanced businesses do, versus 34% of the least digitally sophisticated group of companies. "It's just more difficult to think about any function in isolation because the processes are becoming so integrated," said David Cotteleer, vice president and CIO at Milwaukee, Wisconsin–based Harley-Davidson Inc.

As an example, Cotteleer pointed out that connected vehicles demand a stringent cross-functional approach to design and manufacture. "It's no longer just about product engineering," he said. "It is about software design, system integration, and other elements that fall outside traditional product engineering. Multiple functions in the company are now realizing that what used to be their domain is now also a domain of technology."

At the hospitality company Marriott International Inc., based in Bethesda, Maryland, the team behind the company's push into digital recognized that upgrading mobile apps and the online experience is only half the battle for winning customer loyalty. "We can create the best website on the planet, and we can build the best search campaigns to reach customers," said George Corbin, Marriott's former senior vice president of digital. "But if we can't deliver an exceptional stay, guests won't come back."

At Marriott, coordinating digital innovation with operational excellence required significant collaboration between two groups that were not familiar with each other. Corbin worked closely with his counterparts in operations—spending more time with them than with his own team for a period of time—to ensure that the company could deliver on the promise made by any new app (for example, that a guest who uses a room-service app actually receives the right food at the right time).

General Electric Co.'s transition to digital is similarly forcing the organization to adjust working relationships across functions. In the company's oil and gas business, for instance, traditional sales are big ticket, product-centric, and transactional: Customers purchase machines, as well as parts, maintenance, and repair-service contracts, at fixed prices. Adding machine sensor analytics to the sales mix—a "tiny little sprinkling on top of the deal," said one GE executive—has led to a dramatic shift in the way the sales team collaborates with internal stakeholders.

Selling software solutions "was definitely a change in how our sales personnel approach customer conversations," said Lorenzo Simonelli, former president and CEO of GE Oil & Gas and now president and CEO of Baker Hughes Inc., a GE company based in Houston, Texas. When GE sells an electronic submersible pump, for instance, the equipment sales manager brings along a software application engineer who understands the technical details about how the pump is going to operate in a given environment and how it will interact with the company's IoT platform. With its new focus on digital, GE is changing what it is selling, how it sells, and to whom it sells.

Collaboration with Customers

Pursuing strategies that depend on IoT often requires creating value through collaboration, especially with customers. In a 2016 *MIT SMR* IoT survey of more than 1,400 managers, two-thirds of the respondents who were actively working on IoT projects said they collect data from and/or send data to their customers, suppliers, or competitors. This exchange of device data across organizational borders deepens existing relationships between organizations and encourages new collaborations with customers.

WASH Multifamily Laundry Systems LLC, based in El Segundo, California, is a case in point. Providing service to more than 70,000 locations, the company's extensive network of hundreds of thousands of interconnected washers, dryers, vending machines, and payment systems serves roughly 7 million residents a week.

In the past, WASH would deliver machines to apartment buildings, repair equipment when it broke down, collect quarters, or provide alternative payment systems. Today, WASH also draws on a continuous flow of machine data from suppliers (such as the makers of washers, dryers, and vending equipment), service providers (such as telecommunications providers), and consumers to create and test new services.

For instance, the company is working with its college customers to adjust pricing at peak periods to spread demand, reduce congestion, and improve student experience in dormitories. Individual locations can struggle to run pricing experiments, since all machines must be priced the same at a given location. Random price changes, a valuable component of experiments, run the risk of alienating customers. To help, WASH built an experimentation platform that matches characteristics of a location with similar locations in its network and varies attributes of interest, such as price.

Nedbank Group Ltd., a banking and financial services company based in the Sandton section of Johannesburg, South Africa, used its digital capabilities to collaborate more with customers as it addressed a strategic issue in its card and payments business. In order to grow, the business unit had to identify and commercialize new services for its merchant customers. The bank turned to its massive trove of demographic, geolocation, and transactional data, hoping to give its merchant clients valuable insights about their own businesses.

Developers of the tool, called Market Edge, quickly demonstrated its value to some of Nedbank's largest merchant customers. With the new tool, the South African hardware retailer BUCO discerned patterns in what kinds of customers were visiting which stores and when. Judy Gounden, a group marketing executive at BUCO's parent company, Iliad Africa Ltd., based in Midrand, South Africa, recalled that "when I told a store manager who believed that most of his business was derived from local residents that, in fact, half of his business was coming from residents that lived in a town 10 kilometers away, his eyes went wide and he said, 'How do you know that?' So we shared the data with him."

Talent was a limiting factor in the rollout of Market Edge. Retailers don't always know what to do with raw information.

Technology innovation is another factor driving – and benefiting from – collaborations with customers and other stakeholders.

"We can't just expect a retailer who is very good at knowing what shampoo should be on the shelf to see data and interpret it in a way that makes them change their business," said Chris Wood, Nedbank's head of emerging payments, strategy, and regulation. Collaborating with customers to identify the most relevant and valuable data was essential, but Nedbank had to develop its own team from scratch to support the sales team that typically worked with clients.

Technology innovation is another factor driving—and benefiting from—collaborations with customers and other stakeholders. Increasingly, health care organizations are seeking innovations to improve patient outcomes and reduce costs. Cardinal Health Inc., based in Dublin, Ohio, established an innovation lab to bring together physicians, patients, pharmacists, and providers to understand issues, craft solutions, and try them out. Software developers, for instance, don scrubs and shadow clinicians to get a feel for process flow. Customers and employees regularly propose ideas that are screened and tested using one-week agile sprints. "It's not just about bringing people in," noted Brent Stutz, Cardinal Health's senior vice president of commercial technologies. "It is about getting them out and observing."

Adapting to Increased Collaboration

Digitally advanced companies are more collaborative because they pursue corporate objectives that depend on the effective use of technology, which, in turn, depends on effective collaborations. But increasing collaboration can be fraught: Different functions may exhibit a history of animosity toward one another; individuals with strong egos may not work effectively together; sharing relationships with clients may be anathema for others; and misaligned goals or mistrust can stymie efforts to create shared value with external partners. Overcoming these challenges can mean changing work practices, behavior norms, and metrics of success—in short, adapting essential elements of a company's culture.

At the New York–based financial services company MetLife Inc., Marty Lippert, executive vice president of global technology and operations, said that his company's emphasis on digital has meant a new approach to developing leaders. "One of the top criteria for us today is looking at—and looking for—people who have the skill sets to work cross-functionally across the organization," Lippert said. Working cross-functionally has become so important that the company is training its hiring managers in behavioral-based interviewing skills to ensure that new hires have cross-functional abilities.

Cardinal Health's Stutz stresses that maintaining (rather than just building) a digital culture that supports collaboration can be one of the more demanding challenges. Collaboration needs the right talent. When it comes to hiring for and building a digitally supportive culture, Stutz looks for characteristics such as empathy, problem-solving ability, curiosity, and adaptability. As he put it, "It's not always the smartest person we hire, but the person who is going to be the team player and bring a genuine passion and energy for solving big problems."

8

What's Your Cognitive Technology Strategy?

Thomas H. Davenport and Vikram Mahidhar

Artificial intelligence (AI) and cognitive technologies are burgeoning, but few companies are yet getting value from their investments. The reason, in our view, is that many of the projects companies undertake aren't targeted at important business problems or opportunities. Some projects are simply too ambitious—the technology isn't ready, or the organizational change required is too great.

In short, most organizations don't have a strategy for cognitive technologies. Managers may question whether having a strategy for a specific technology is necessary, but in the case of cognitive technology the justification seems clear. A 2018 survey of senior executives in 60 large companies by Boston, Massachusetts–based consulting firm NewVantage Partners, where one of us (Tom Davenport) is a fellow, found that 72% of respondents saw cognitive technologies as the force most likely to disrupt their companies over the next decade (up from 44% in 2017), and 93% said their companies were already investing in cognitive technologies.[1]

Similarly, a 2017 survey of 300 C-suite and other senior executives by Genpact, a global professional services firm (where

Vikram Mahidhar works), found that 96% of AI leaders—
companies that achieve significant business outcomes from AI—
believe AI will transform their workforce, but only 38% said their
companies currently provide employees with reskilling options.[2]

The size of both the opportunity and the disruptive threat
of cognitive technologies makes cognitive strategy different
from other technology strategies—say, e-commerce. Cognitive
technology stands to be transformational. Driving the kind of
widespread organizational change it will require won't be easy,
especially when it comes to implications for the workforce.
Companies need to give careful consideration to how boldly
they will step forward into the cognitive world and how much
risk they are willing to take on. Developing a coherent cognitive
strategy—and a means to fund it—can give companies a distinct
competitive advantage. The first critical step in this process is to
define the purpose, goals, and key components of such a strategy. We aim to help you lay this groundwork in this article.

How to Approach Cognitive Strategy

Broadly speaking, cognitive technologies employ capabilities—
including knowledge, perception, judgment, and the where-
withal to accomplish specific tasks—that were once the exclusive
domain of humans. The question for managers is where and
how to apply them. Should you use them to create new products or offerings? To boost product performance? To optimize
internal business operations? To improve customer processes? To
reduce head count? To free up workers to be more creative? How
companies go about applying cognitive technologies needs to be
driven by the specifics of the company's strategy.

The goal isn't to develop a new business strategy but to devise well-informed actions that align with existing business goals. For many companies, the cognitive strategy will result in a series of pilots, proofs of concept, and deployments of cognitive tools in various parts of the business. It will also provide a mechanism for reskilling managers and employees to lead and run a cognitive-driven business.

One obvious area of interest is how to use cognitive technology to create new offerings that support top-line growth. A leader in this pursuit is General Electric Co., which has developed powerful tools that can digitally represent large machines such as jet engines, gas turbines, and windmills for the purpose of monitoring their performance. As sensors collect data representing conditions such as heat, vibration, and noise, the tools— referred to as "digital twins"—can diagnose faults, identify performance trends, and predict maintenance needs, thereby reducing unplanned downtime. In addition to using the capability to optimize performance of specific pieces of equipment, companies can use such a capability more broadly to manage entire plants or fleets of aircraft or equipment, and to spot new revenue sources.

In addition to new products and services, increased customer personalization that arises out of cognitive technology can yield revenue increases. Telecommunications company Verizon Wireless Inc., for example, having recently suffered revenue declines, decided to invest in personalized marketing. Using intelligent agents that integrated hundreds of variables, including usage of current offerings and calls for service, it was able to develop combinations of products and target promotions to customers in specific zip codes that reversed the declines. For customers with specific phones and usage patterns, it created a "next best offer" program and an automatic upgrade aimed at customers who craved the newest phone.[3]

Process optimization, too, is a fertile area for cognitive solutions, thanks to the availability of data and the inefficiency inherent in many labor-intensive processes. A large US consumer product manufacturer, for example, recently automated the audit process for paying retailers for trade promotions. It trained a machine to read and match unstructured text in contracts, invoices, and point-of-sales data, reducing its audit processing cost by about 60%. With the improved ability to identify erroneous charges (for example, bills from retailers for promotion allowances for goods that were not actually ordered), it was able to increase profits by $20 million annually.

Although some companies have pursued fairly narrow cognitive strategies, others have been more ambitious. Efforts made by Procter & Gamble Co., for example, have highlighted three key components.[4] The first one is to use machine learning to ensure that spending in areas such as trade promotion and digital advertising is efficiently allocated and targeted. The second is to use data (including new external data sets) to develop precision marketing models and programs for consumers. The third is to develop platforms and applications that help consumers use P&G products more effectively in their homes and lives. A good example is the Olay Skin Advisor, an image-processing system that can evaluate the condition of a woman's facial skin from a photo. The findings can help her choose the most suitable Olay products.

Key Levers of Cognitive Strategy

Companies we have worked with are developing cognitive technology strategies that address a variety of issues, including content, technology components, people, change management, and ambitions.

Leveraging content   Companies that own proprietary content, be it data or knowledge, should look for ways to incorporate that content in their products and processes, as well as in a cognitive system. This requires finding or creating a "knowledge graph" the company wants to license or own. This is particularly critical for natural language processing applications, such as intelligent agents or chatbots. A knowledge graph describes the relationships between key entities and terms used in the business and in its relationships. Google Inc. pioneered the idea of the knowledge graph when it began collecting billions of facts about internet searches and representing how they relate to each other on a graph.[5] Other companies, such as IBM Corp. in its Watson division, have obtained their knowledge graphs from outside partners or through acquisitions (as IBM did through its purchase of The Weather Co. LLC for weather data). Although Watson is known for ingesting medical journals, perhaps it's more noteworthy for its ability to convert content into "question/answer pairs" that can be used in interactions with clinicians.[6]

Companies should think carefully before turning over content ownership and usage rights regarding core customers and products, or proprietary process information, to other organizations—even if the would-be users are able to add significant value to what they receive. Unless the information relates to tactical processes like facilities management or maintenance, companies should treat their information as a valuable corporate asset and seek ways to add value themselves. A pharmaceuticals company, for example, will probably want to own the content and models related to drug development, though it may be less

intent on owning the knowledge graph for clinical trial processes, which are often outsourced anyway.

Technology components   Cognitive technology isn't one technology but a collection of them. It includes statistical machine
learning, neural networks, and natural language processing and
generation. Beyond selecting specific technologies, companies
need to decide whether to build or buy the capabilities, whether
to use proprietary or open-source software, whether to use one
vendor's tools or employ "best of breed," and whether to use
stand-alone applications or a broad platform.

There are no right answers—only decisions to make about
what aligns best with an organization's capabilities, business
strategy, and overall cognitive strategy.[7] Organizations with volu-
minous and rapidly changing structured data about customers
may find that machine learning provides insight into customer
preferences. However, if the need is to identify and sort unstructured information (such as sounds and images), deep-learning
neural networks will work better.

Clearly, some companies are more knowledgeable about the
powers of cognitive technology than others. Procter & Gamble
and American Express Co., for example, have been involved
with artificial intelligence since the 1980s. They have the ability
to build their own cognitive applications and cobble together
solutions using open-source tools. For companies with less experience and less-seasoned developers and data scientists, undertaking such challenges would be unthinkable.[8] Those without
internal expertise can work with expert analysts, IT professionals, and data scientists. And as the field develops, companies with little cognitive technology experience will have other
options as well. Increasingly, mainstream applications such as

Einstein, from Salesforce.com Inc., are embedding cognitive capabilities that do things like allow users to identify the best sales leads. It ranks leads according to their probability of closing based on factors drawn from past sales data (such as whether or not the lead received a product demo). SAP SE and Oracle Corp., for their part, are embedding cognitive technologies into their enterprise resource planning systems. Implementing these functions requires little technical sophistication.

Companies lacking experience but with a desire to build numerous cognitive applications may want to use a cognitive platform that includes a variety of tools. IBM's Watson, which uses a range of application programming interfaces that enable companies to build software applications, is perhaps the best known. In addition, large technology vendors such as Amazon, Google, and Microsoft offer a variety of machine learning algorithms on their platforms, most of which are open source. Proprietary vendors increasingly offer platforms with multiple programs that can be assembled to solve particular problems. While the capabilities of cognitive technologies are evolving quickly, every platform needs integration. In choosing a platform, the most important criterion should be whether it helps you address the types of problems you want to solve in the near term. You should also ensure that the technology you choose can both help you solve cognitive problems and assist you in deploying them into production systems and processes.

People A key question for any organization seeking to pursue cognitive initiatives is how to find people who can do the work. Organizations have struggled in recent years with similar concerns about finding quantitative analysts and data scientists. The good news: An increasing number of universities' graduates are broadly educated in analytics and data science. The bad news: Not many of these graduates have been trained in cognitive technologies or specific methods. Similarly, there is a shortage of faculty who are sufficiently familiar with cognitive technologies to teach about them—and many of those who are deeply knowledgeable have been recruited out of the classroom to work for tech companies.

Nevertheless, companies need access to people with deep domain knowledge and awareness of cognitive technologies: Without such expertise, the organization's cognitive strategies will be based on neither. Those involved in strategic planning for cognitive technologies should be familiar with the major types of cognitive technology, how they can be applied, and how they might integrate with other information technologies. They should be able to communicate with managers in nontechnical terms, and they should be familiar with the key issues of the business and its current strategic direction. They should also have an understanding of the particular business domains to which cognitive technology will be applied.

In determining the appropriate people strategies, the choices are much the same as they are for the technologies themselves: Should you buy, build, or rent? To "buy" people, you will probably need to be located in a city with a large pool of technology talent and be prepared to offer attractive pay, stock options, and benefits. It will help if your company is taking on some interesting challenges.

To "build" people, you will need to train them in the necessary skills. Cisco Systems Inc., the networking hardware company based in San Jose, California, has been a leader for years in training and retraining employees in data science and cognitive skills. Through its distance-learning program for aspiring

Companies need access to people with deep domain knowledge and awareness of cognitive technologies.

data scientists, it has trained several hundred data scientists who work for the company.[9]

The third option, "renting" people who work for consulting firms and who are already trained in the use of cognitive applications, is widely practiced by companies that lack the in-house expertise to build applications. This approach can work if the vendor or consulting firm has sufficiently well-trained people (this cannot be taken for granted). Companies interested in building longer-term capabilities in the cognitive space may find it useful to use a combination of employees and outside people.

No matter which people strategy you choose, it may be helpful to begin with a management education program for the executives who will ultimately make strategy decisions. Indeed, perhaps the most important aspect of a people strategy is helping senior executives and business unit leaders rethink how the businesses will work with cognitive technology. Although companies should be concerned with how they will develop cognitive applications, they also need individuals with business analysis skills and the ability to frame business problems to identify what technologies are appropriate to address them. Design-thinking skills play an important role as well—both for user interfaces and for the business processes in which the cognitive technologies will be applied.

At a large US bank's business- and investment-banking unit, for example, the senior management team wanted the business unit to explore new financial technologies, including a series of cognitive technologies, machine learning among them. The executives evaluated several vendors to determine the best way to familiarize the bank and its managers with the technology. The vendor they chose developed a training program for about 40 managers, several of whom went on to become active supporters of new applications in their specific business areas. The applications included one that identifies business customers who are most likely to prepay loans and another that extracts relevant information from public data about privately held businesses.

Change management Projects employing cognitive technologies are not just about technological change. Those that go beyond the pilot or proof-of-concept stage are also intended to help transform organizational culture, behavior, and attitudes. These are not small challenges, especially given the apparent threat to people's jobs. Since cognitive technologies often involve the management or application of knowledge, these projects can be extremely threatening to knowledge workers. It is critical to address their concerns head on, as the threat appears largely overblown.

In fact, in most of the nearly 200 cognitive projects we have studied, we have seen minimal layoffs. Take medical imaging. For years, there have been imaging systems based on cognitive technology that can detect potential cancers. Several studies have found that such systems can provide more accurate and reliable diagnoses than human radiologists.[10] However, the new systems have not yet replaced radiologists, nor are they likely to do so any time soon. The technology isn't fully proven, and the integration with daily clinical processes will take many years.

Describing how cognitive technologies can provide improvements over the status quo, such as substantially increasing capacity or accomplishing tasks that weren't possible before, will help organizations generate employee support in the transformation process.

Ambitions Finally, there's the question of how ambitious you should be. Some organizations pursue highly ambitious initiatives that have the potential to be game-changers. Others choose more modest goals—adding an intelligent agent as an experimental new channel to customers or automating a set of tasks. There is no right answer to the question of ambition. That said, there are few examples of organizations that have succeeded in bringing about radical transformations with cognitive technologies, while there are many examples of organizations successfully going after "low-hanging fruit."

In recent years, MD Anderson Cancer Center, in Houston, Texas, has pursued both approaches in different parts of the organization, with varying results. In 2012, the organization began an innovation project it actually referred to as a "moonshot," in which it used IBM's Watson to diagnose and treat certain forms of cancer. In 2017, after investing more than $60 million, the hospital put the project on hold.[11] It was not able to treat patients successfully yet, and it had not been integrated at all with the hospital's electronic medical record system.

During the same time frame, a group within the IT function at MD Anderson employed cognitive technologies on more mundane tasks. These included making hotel and restaurant recommendations for patients' families, determining which patients needed help paying bills, and launching an automated "cognitive help desk" for addressing staff IT problems. Another group used machine learning to analyze cancer treatments for patients with particular genomes. These projects have been successful, and more are underway.

MD Anderson's experience with cognitive projects offers lessons to anyone weighing cognitive initiatives. Although there are circumstances in which highly ambitious projects may be appropriate, in our view they are best suited to settings where the technology has been tested, the organization has already had success with large-scale IT-driven transformation, and senior managers are fully on board. For most companies, the best approach is to develop a series of more modest applications in the same general area of the business (say, improving customer relationships) that together have the potential to have a substantial effect on the business. That way, each element will be relatively low risk, and the company will have time to ease into a transformation.

Cognitive technology is not a fad. In the eyes of many managers, it is the most disruptive technology on the horizon. Investors seem to agree. Leaders need to begin laying the groundwork for their cognitive strategies and begin implementing cognitive technologies, or risk being left behind.

Companies should expect their established competitors to eventually adopt cognitive technologies, and be aware that many are doing so now. However, a bigger threat may come from tech-centric players who aren't afraid to develop business models around technology. The Googles and Amazons of the world have aggressively adopted AI and are rapidly moving into new business domains. Companies should brace themselves for a wave of similar threats from new ventures built on cognitive technology from the ground up. Companies that ignore the power of these technologies and the business processes and models they enable will be at a considerable disadvantage as we move rapidly into a cognitively enabled world.

Shift Up

9

Building a More Intelligent Enterprise

Paul J. H. Schoemaker and Philip E. Tetlock

To succeed in the long run, businesses need to create and leverage some kind of sustainable competitive edge. This advantage can still derive from such traditional sources as scale-driven lower cost, proprietary intellectual property, highly motivated employees, or farsighted strategic leaders. But in the knowledge economy, strategic advantages will increasingly depend on a shared capacity to make superior judgments and choices.

Intelligent enterprises today are being shaped by two distinct forces. The first is the growing power of computers and big data, which provide the foundation for operations research, forecasting models, and artificial intelligence (AI). The second is our growing understanding of human judgment, reasoning, and choice. Decades of research has yielded deep insights into what humans do well or poorly.[1]

About the Research

This article combines insights from strategy, organization theory, human judgment, predictive analytics, and management science. The ideas described in several of the five methods are based on what we learned in working with companies, as well as from our involvement in a geopolitical and economic forecasting tournament that ran from 2011 through 2015, funded by the Intelligence Advanced Research Projects Activity (IARPA). This tournament required the entrants to develop probabilistic forecasts, which were then scored based on actual outcomes. Five academic research teams recruited a total of 20,000 forecasters to participate in four yearly rounds of the IARPA tournament. The official performance metric for each team was its cumulative Brier score, a measure that assesses probabilistic accuracy. The scores were compared across questions, teams, and experimental conditions. Phil Tetlock and Barbara Mellers, the I. George Heyman University Professor at the University of Pennsylvania, led the Good Judgment Project team, with Paul Schoemaker serving as one of several advisers. This team won the competition.

In this article, we will examine how managers can combine human intelligence with technology-enabled insights to make smarter choices in the face of uncertainty and complexity. Integrating the two streams of knowledge is not easy, but once management teams learn how to blend them, the advantages can be substantial. A company that can make the right decision three times out of five as opposed to 2.8 out of five can gain an upper hand over its competitors. Although this performance gap may seem trivial, small differences can lead to big statistical advantages over time. In tennis, for example, if a player has a 55% versus 45% edge on winning points throughout the match, he or she will have a greater than 90% chance of winning the best of three sets.[2]

To help your company gain such a cumulative advantage in business, we have identified five strategic capabilities that intelligent enterprises can use to outsmart the competition through better judgments and wise choices. Thanks to their use of big data and predictive analytics, many companies have begun cultivating some of these capabilities already.[3] But few have systematically integrated the power of computers with the latest understanding of the human mind. For managers looking to gain an advantage on competitors, we see opportunities today to do the following:

- **Find the strategic edge.** In assessing past organizational forecasts, home in on areas where improving subjective predictions can really move the needle.
- **Run prediction tournaments.** Discover the best forecasting methods by encouraging competition, experimentation, and innovation among teams.
- **Model the experts in your midst.** Identify the people internally who have demonstrated superior insights into key business areas, and leverage their wisdom using simple linear models.
- **Experiment with artificial intelligence.** Go beyond simple linear models. Use deep neural nets in limited task domains to outperform human experts.
- **Change the way the organization operates.** Promote an exploratory culture that continually looks for better ways to combine the capabilities of humans and machines.

Find the Strategic Edge

The starting point for becoming an intelligent enterprise is learning to allocate analytical effort where it will most pay off—in other words, being strategic about which problems you decide to tackle head-on. The sweet spot for intelligent enterprises is where hard data and soft judgment can be productively combined. On one side, this zone is bounded by problems that philosopher Karl Popper dubbed "clocklike" because of their deterministic regularities; on the other side, it is bounded by problems he dubbed "cloudlike" because of their uncertainty.[4]

Clocklike problems are tractable and stable, and they can be defined by past experience (as in actuarial tables or credit reports). Statistical prediction models can shine here. Human judgment operates on the sidelines, although it still plays a role under unusual conditions (such as assessing the impact of new medical advances on life expectancies). Cloudlike problems (for example, assigning probabilities to global warming causing megafloods in Miami in 2025 or ascertaining whether intelligent life exists on other planets) are far murkier. However, what's most critical in such cases is the knowledge base of experts and, more importantly, their nuanced appreciation of what they do and don't know. The sweet spot for managers lies in combining the

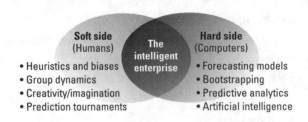

Finding the Sweet Spot

To create a more intelligent enterprise, executives need to leverage the strengths of both humans and computers in order to produce superior judgments. That will require a sophisticated understanding of both human decision making (the "soft side") and evolving technology-enabled capabilities (the "hard side"). By avoiding judgmental biases that often distort human information processing and by recognizing the precarious assumptions on which statistical models sometimes rest, the analytical whole can occasionally become more than the sum of its parts.

strengths of computers and algorithms with seasoned human judgment and judicious questioning.

Creating a truly intelligent enterprise is neither quick nor simple. Some of what we recommend will seem counterintuitive and requires training. Breakthroughs in cognitive psychology over the past few decades have attuned many sophisticated leaders to the biases and traps of undisciplined thinking.[5] However, few companies have been able to transform these insights into game-changing practices that make their business much smarter. Companies that perform data mining remain blissfully unaware of the quirks and foibles that shape their analysts' hunches. At the same time, executive teams advancing opinions are seldom asked to defend their views in depth. In most cases, outcomes of judgments or decisions are rarely reviewed against the starting assumptions. There is a clear opportunity to raise a company's IQ by both improving corporate decision-making processes and leveraging data and technology tools.

Run Prediction Tournaments

One promising method for creating better corporate forecasts involves using what are known as prediction tournaments to surface the people and approaches that generate the best judgments in a given domain. The idea of a prediction tournament is to incentivize participants to predict what they think will happen, translate their assessments into probabilities, and then track which predictions proved most accurate. In a prediction tournament, there is no benefit in being overly positive or overly negative, or in engaging in strategic gaming against rivals. The job of tournament organizers is to develop a set of relevant questions and then attract participants to provide answers.

One organization that has used prediction tournaments effectively is the Intelligence Advanced Research Projects Activity (IARPA). It operates within the US Office of the Director of National Intelligence and is responsible for running high-risk, high-return research on how to improve intelligence analysis. In 2011, IARPA invited five research teams to compete to develop the best methods of boosting the accuracy of human probability judgments of geopolitical events. The topics covered the gamut, from possible Eurozone exits to the direction of the North Korean nuclear program. One of the authors (Phil Tetlock) co-led a team known as the Good Judgment Project,[6] which won this tournament by ignoring folklore and conducting field experiments to discover what really drives forecasting accuracy. Four key factors emerged as critical to successful predictions:[7]

- Identifying the attributes of consistently superior forecasters, including their greater curiosity, open-mindedness, and willingness to test the idea that forecasting might be a skill that can be cultivated and is worth cultivating;
- Training people in techniques for avoiding common cognitive biases such as overconfidence and overweighting evidence that reinforces their preconceptions;
- Creating stimulating work environments that encourage the best performers to engage in collaborative teamwork and offer guidance on how to avoid groupthink by practicing techniques like precision questioning and constructive confrontation;
- Devising better statistical methods to extract wisdom from crowds by, for example, giving more weight to forecasters with better track records and more diverse viewpoints.[8]

Based on our experience, the biggest benefit of prediction tournaments within organizations is their power to accelerate learning cycles. Companies can accelerate learning by adhering to several principles.

- The first principle involves careful record keeping. By keeping accurate records, it is harder to misremember earlier forecasts, one's own, and those of others. This is a critical counterweight to the self-serving tendency to say "I knew it all along," as well as the inclination to deny credit to rivals "who didn't have a clue."

- Second, by making it difficult for contestants to misremember, tournaments force people to confront their failures and the other side's successes. Typically, one's first response to failure is denial. Tournaments prompt people to become more reflective, to engage in a pattern of thinking known as preemptive self-criticism; they encourage participants to consider ways in which they might have been deeply wrong.

- Third, tournaments produce winners, which naturally awakens curiosity in others about how the superior results were achieved. Teams are encouraged to experiment and improve their methods all along.

- Fourth, the scoring in prediction tournaments is clear to all involved up front.[9] This creates a sense of fair competition among all.

Until recently, there was little published research that training in probabilistic reasoning and cognitive debiasing could improve forecasting of complex real-world events.[10] Academics felt that eliminating cognitive illusions was nearly impossible for people to achieve on their own.[11] The IARPA tournaments revealed, however, that customized training of only a few hours can deliver benefits. Specifically, training exercises involving behavioral decision theory—from statistical reasoning to scenario planning and group dynamics—hold great promise for improving managers' decision-making skills. At companies we have worked with, the training typically involves individual and group exercises to demonstrate cognitive biases, video tutorials on topics such as scenario planning, and customized business simulations.

Model the Experts in Your Midst

Another way to create a more intelligent enterprise is to model the knowledge of expert employees so it can be leveraged more effectively and objectively. This can be done using a technique known in decision-making research as bootstrapping.[12] An early example of bootstrapping research in decision psychology involved a study that explored what was on the minds of agricultural experts who were judging the quality of corn at a wholesale auction where farmers brought their crops.[13] The researchers asked the corn judges to rate 500 ears of corn to predict their eventual prices in the marketplace. These expert judges considered a variety of factors, including the length and circumference of each ear, the weight of the kernels, the filling of the kernels at the tip, the blistering, and the starchiness. The researchers then created a simple scoring model based on cues that judges claimed were most important in driving their own predictions. Both the judges and the researchers expected the simple additive models to do much worse than the predictions of seasoned experts. But to everyone's surprise, the models that mimicked the judges' strategies nearly always performed better than the judges themselves.

Similar surprises occurred when banks introduced computer models several decades ago to assist in making loan decisions. Few loan officers believed that a simplified model of their professional judgments could make better predictions than experienced loan officers could make. The sense was that consumer loans contained many subjective factors that only savvy loan officers could properly assess, so there was skepticism about whether distilling intuitive expertise into a simple formula could help new loan officers learn faster. But here, too, the models performed better than most loan experts.[14] In other fields, from predicting the performance of newly hired salespeople to the bankruptcy risks of companies to the life expectancies of terminally ill cancer patients, the experience has been essentially the same.[15] Even though experts usually possess deep knowledge, they often do not make good predictions.[16]

When humans make predictions, wisdom gets mixed with "random noise." By noise, we mean the inconsistencies that creep into human judgments due to fatigue, boredom, and other vagaries of being human.[17] Bootstrapping, which incorporates expert judgment into a decision-making model, eliminates such inconsistencies while preserving the expert's insights.[18] But this does not occur when human judgment is employed on its own. In a classic medical study, for instance, nine radiologists were presented with information from 96 cases of suspected stomach ulcers and asked to evaluate them for the likelihood of a malignancy.[19] A week later, the radiologists were shown the same information, although this time in a different order. In 23% of the cases, the second assessments differed from their first.[20] None of the radiologists was completely consistent across their two assessments, and some were inconsistent nearly half of the time.

In fields ranging from medicine to finance, scores of studies have shown that replacing experts with models of experts produces superior judgments.[21] In most cases, the bootstrapping model performed better than experts on their own.[22] Nonetheless, bootstrapping models tend to be rather rudimentary in that human experts are usually needed to identify the factors that matter most in making predictions. Humans are also instrumental in assigning scores to the predictor variables (such as judging the strength of recommendation letters for college applications or the overall health of patients in medical cases). What's more, humans are good at spotting when the model is getting out of date and needs updating.

Bootstrapping lacks the high-tech pizzazz of deep neural nets in artificial intelligence. However, it remains one of the most compelling demonstrations of the potential benefits of combining the powers of models and humans, including the value of expert intuition.[23] It also raises the question of whether permitting more human intervention (for example, when a doctor has information that goes beyond the model) can yield further benefit. In such circumstances, there is the risk that humans want to override the model too often since they will deem too many cases as special or unique.[24] One way to incorporate additional expert perspective is to allow the expert (for example, a loan officer or a doctor) a limited number of overrides to the model's recommendation.

A field study by marketing scholars tested the effects of combining humans and models in the retail sector.[25] The researchers studied two different situations: (1) predictions by professional buyers of catalog sales for fashion merchandise, and (2) brand

In fields ranging from medicine to finance, scores of studies have shown that replacing experts with models of experts produces superior judgments.

managers' predictions for coupon-redemption rates. Once the researchers had the actual results in hand, they compared the results to the forecasts. Then they tested how different combinations of humans and models might perform the same tasks. The researchers found that in both the catalog sales and coupon-redemption settings, an even balance between the human and the model yielded the best predictions.

Experiment with Artificial Intelligence

Bootstrapping uses a simple input–output approach to modeling expertise without delving into process models of human reasoning. Accordingly, bootstrapping can be augmented by AI technologies that allow for more complex relationships among variables drawn from human insights or from mining big data sets.

Deeper cognitive insights drove computer modeling of master chess players back in the early days of AI. But modeling human thinking—with all its biases—has its limits; often, computers are able to develop an edge simply by using superior computing power to study old data. This is how IBM Corp.'s Deep Blue supercomputer managed to beat the world chess champion Garry Kasparov in 1997. Today AI covers various types of machine intelligence, including computer vision, natural language comprehension, robotics, and machine learning. However, AI still lacks a broad intelligence of the kind humans have that can cut across domains. Human experts thus remain important whenever contextual intelligence, creativity, or broad knowledge of the world is needed.

Humans simplify the complex world around them by using various cognitive mechanisms, including pattern matching and storytelling, to connect new stimuli to the mental models in

their heads.[26] When psychologists studied jurors in mock mur-
der trials, for example, they found that jurors built stories from
the limited data available and then processed new information
to reinforce the initial storyline.[27] The risk is that humans get
trapped in their own initial stories and then start to weigh con-
firming evidence more heavily than information that doesn't fit
their internal narratives.[28] People often see patterns that are not
really there, or they fail to see that new data requires changing
the storyline.[29]

Human experts typically provide signal, noise, and bias in
unknown proportions, which makes it difficult to disentangle
these three components in field settings.[30] Whether humans or
computers have the upper hand depends on many factors, including whether the tasks being undertaken are familiar or unique.
When tasks are familiar and much data is available, computers
will likely beat humans by being data-driven and highly consistent from one case to the next. But when tasks are unique (where
creativity may matter more) and when data overload is not a
problem for humans, humans will likely have an advantage.

One might think that humans have an advantage over models
in understanding dynamically complex domains, with feedback
loops, delays, and instability. But psychologists have examined
how people learn about complex relationships in simulated
dynamic environments (for example, a computer game modeling an airline's strategic decisions or those of an electronics company managing a new product).[31] Even after receiving extensive
feedback after each round of play, the human subjects improved
only slowly over time and failed to beat simple computer models. This raises questions about how much human expertise is
desirable when building models for complex dynamic environments. The best way to find out is to compare how well humans

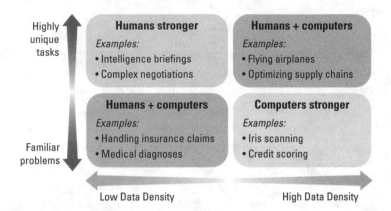

The Comparative Advantages of Humans and Computers

Whether humans or computers have the upper hand depends on many factors, including whether the tasks being undertaken are familiar or unique. When tasks are familiar and much data is available, computers will likely beat humans by being data-driven and highly consistent. Although artificial intelligence is advancing rapidly, a general rule of thumb is that when tasks are unique and when data overload is not a problem for humans, humans likely have an advantage. In many situations, the strongest performance comes from humans and computers working together.

and models do in specific domains and perhaps develop hybrid models that integrate different approaches.

AI systems have been rapidly improving in recent years. Traditional expert systems used rule-based models that mimicked human expertise by employing if–then rules (for example, "If symptoms X, Y, and Z are present, then try solution no. 5 first.").[32] Most AI applications today, however, use network structures, which search for new linkages between input variables and output results. In deep neural nets used in AI applications, the aim is to analyze very large data sets so that the system can discover complex relationships and refine them whenever more feedback is provided. AI is thriving thanks to deep neural nets developed for particular tasks, including playing games like chess and Go, driving cars, synthesizing speech, and translating language.[33]

Companies should be closely tracking the development of AI applications to determine which aspects are worthiest of adoption and adaptation in their industry. Bridgewater Associates LP, a hedge fund firm based in Westport, Connecticut, is an example of a company already experimenting with AI. Bridgewater Associates is developing various algorithmic models designed to automate much of the management of the firm by capturing insights from the best minds in the organization.[34]

Artificial general intelligence of the kind that most humans exhibit is emerging more slowly than targeted AI applications. Artificial general intelligence remains a rather small portion of current AI research, with the high-commercial-value work focused on narrow domains such as speech recognition, object classification in photographs, or handwriting analysis.[35] Still, the idea of artificial general intelligence has captured the popular imagination, with movies depicting real-life robots capable of performing a broad range of complex tasks. In the near term, the best predictive business systems will likely deploy a complex layering of humans and machines in order to garner the comparative advantages of each. Unlike machines, human experts possess general intelligence that is naturally sensitive to real-world contexts and is capable of deep self-reflection and moral judgments.

Change the Way the Organization Operates

In our view, the most powerful decision-support systems are hybrids that fuse multiple technologies together. Such decision aids will become increasingly common, expanding beyond narrow applications such as sales forecasting to providing a foundation for broader systems such as IBM's Watson, which, among other things, helps doctors make complex medical diagnoses. Over time, we expect the underlying technologies to become more and more sophisticated, eventually reaching the point where decision-support devices will be on par with, or better than, most human advisers.

As machines become more sophisticated, humans and organizations will advance as well. To eliminate the excessive noise that often undermines human judgments in many organizations and to amplify the signals that truly matter, we recommend two strategies. First, organizations can record people's judgments in "prediction banks" to monitor their accuracy over time.[36] Rather than being overly general, predictions should be clear and crisp so they can be unambiguously scored ex post (without any wiggle room). Second, once managers accumulate personal performance scores in the prediction bank, their track record can help determine their "reputational capital" (which might determine how much weight their view gets in future decisions). Ray Dalio, founder of Bridgewater Associates, has been moving in this direction. He has developed a set of rules and management principles to create a culture that records, scores, and evaluates judgments on an ongoing basis, with high transparency and incentives for personal improvement.[37]

Truly intelligent enterprises will blend the soft side of human judgment, including its known frailties and biases, with the hard side of big data and business analytics to create competitive advantages for companies competing in knowledge economies. From an organizational perspective, the type of transformation we envision will require focusing on three factors. The first involves strategic focus. Leaders will need to determine what kind of intelligence edge they want to develop. For example, do they want to develop superior human judgment under uncertainty, or do they want to push the frontiers of automation? Second, companies will need to focus on building the mindsets, skills, habits, and rewards that can convert judgmental acumen into better calibrated subjective probabilities. Third, organizations will need to promote cultural and process transformations to give employees the confidence to speak truth to power, since the overall aim is to experiment with approaches that challenge conventional wisdom.[38] All this will require changing incentives and, where necessary, breaking down silos so that information can easily flow to where it is most needed.

Having discussed how to improve the science of prediction, it seems fitting to examine the future of forecasting itself. For the sake of comparison, it's worth noting that medicine emerged very rapidly from the time when bloodletting was common to a more scientific approach based on control groups, placebos, and evidence-based research. Currently, the field of subjective prediction is moving beyond its own black magic, thanks to advances in cognitive science. Given how often forecasting methods still fail, we will need to pay attention to outcome-based approaches that rely on experiments and field studies to unearth the best strategies.

Despite ongoing challenges, the science of subjective forecasting has been steadily getting better, even as the external world has become more complex. From wisdom-of-crowd approaches and prediction markets to forecasting tournaments, big data and business analytics, and artificial intelligence, there is much hope about identifying the best approaches.[39] However, there is confusion about how to improve subjective prediction. For example,

Organizations will need to promote cultural and process transformations to give employees the confidence to speak truth to power.

insurance underwriters are still struggling to properly price risks posed by terrorism, global warming, and geopolitical turmoil.[40]

The cognitive science revolution holds both promise and challenge for business leaders. For most companies, the devil will be in the details: which human versus machine approaches to apply to which topics and how to combine the various approaches. Sorting all this out will not be easy, because people and machines think in such different ways. But there is often a common analytical goal and point of comparison when dealing with tasks where foresight matters: assigning well-calibrated probability judgments to events of commercial or political significance. We have focused on real-world forecasting expressed in terms of subjective probabilities because such judgments can be objectively scored later once the outcomes are known. Scoring is more complicated with other important tasks where humans and models can be symbiotically combined, such as making strategic choices. However, once an organization starts to embrace hybrid approaches for making subjective probability estimates and keeps improving them, it can develop a sustainable strategic intelligence advantage over rivals.

The authors thank Rob Adams, Barbara A. Mellers, Nanda Ramanujam, and J. Edward Russo for their helpful feedback on earlier drafts.

10

Creating Management Processes Built for Change

Christopher G. Worley, Thomas Williams, and Edward E. Lawler III

The word "agility" has entered the business lexicon like few other terms in recent memory.[1] Today's strategists extol the importance of strategic agility and resilience. IT professionals talk about the need for agile software development. Yet even as agility is mentioned more often and in more management contexts,[2] we believe that the core concept is misunderstood. Agility refers to an organization's ability to make timely, effective, and sustained changes that maintain superior performance.[3]

An essential feature of agility is repeatability. Agile organizations continuously adjust to changing circumstances by, for example, launching new products or eliminating old ones, entering new markets or exiting underperforming ones, or building new capabilities. This requires management processes that can support adaptability over time.

Agility Routines and Management Processes

To develop our ideas on agility, we studied performance data from the largest public global companies in 22 industries between 1980 and 2012. We also administered strategic change and organizational design surveys in more than 50 companies. We sought to understand the factors that explained sustained levels of high performance and concluded that organizational agility required four routines:

- The *strategizing* routine establishes the purpose, direction, and market position of the organization, and supports what management scholars James O'Toole and Warren Bennis referred to as a "culture of candor" that expects organization members to challenge the status quo;[4]

- The *perceiving* routine connects organizations to their external environment; they can accurately sense and interpret relevant shifts better than their peers do;

- The *testing* routine encourages organizations to experiment with different ideas, allowing them to learn on a continuous basis;

- And, finally, the *implementing* routine facilitates day-to-day changes in products, operations, structures, and systems, but more importantly, orchestrates the development of new capabilities, business models, and strategies.

About the Research

Building on prior adaptability, resilience, ambidexterity, leadership, and change research, the ideas presented in this article are the result of a research program exploring two questions. First, are high levels of business performance sustainable over the long term? Second, if so, which factors are most important?

To answer the first question, we used Compustat's North America Fundamentals Annual database to gather performance data for the largest public companies in 22 industries between 1980 and 2012.[5] We viewed the data directly, year by year and over time, to understand the patterns of performance. Ultimately, we took a manager's, rather than an investor's, view of performance and measured relative profitability within an industry peer group. When each company's annual rate of return on assets (ROA) or, for financial services companies, return on equity (ROE) was compared to its industry average, we found three performance patterns: (1) companies that outperformed their peers at least 80% of the time (16% of the sample), (2) companies that under-performed their industry peers 80% or more of the time (18% of the sample), and (3) companies that oscillated between periods of success and failure (66% of the sample).

To answer the second question, we conducted structured manage-ment interviews and administered a survey in more than 50 companies representing all three performance patterns. The interview and survey questions were based on an extensive review of the strategic change, adaptation, and organization design research. We hypothesized that it was management's ability to anticipate and effectively adapt to changes in their competitive environments over the 32-year period that deter-mined performance.

We developed the perspective that agility is a capability comprising four routines: strategizing, perceiving, testing, and implementing. High-performing companies possessed three or four of the routines and were more likely to have shared leadership philosophies, robust strategic plan-ning cycles, transparent information systems, flexible resource alloca-tion systems, and externally focused structures.

Routines and capabilities allow organizations to get things done reliably and repeatedly.[6] Some, such as lowering costs or improving quality, enable organizations to keep pace with a changing world. Others, such as designing superior customer experiences or reducing the time it takes to achieve profitability in new markets, can provide distinct advantages. The agility rou-tines play the critical role of making continuous change possible and profitable.

However, the four routines are not enough. Management processes—the fundamentals of planning, organizing, controlling, and motivating, as described by Peter Drucker, Henry Mintzberg, and others—operationalize routines and capabilities. They align goals throughout the organization, develop capital and operating budgets, define roles and responsibilities, hold people accountable for results, and reward employees in a systematic fashion. They are the nuts and bolts that make agility possible.

To support agility, all management processes need to be designed well, and *some* of them must be designed for change. Well-designed management processes are fit for purpose: They support the execution of existing strategies and capabilities. However, executives in agile organizations are suspicious of management bromides that support overly efficient and unnecessarily complex management processes in service of defending a competitive position. They see these as futile attempts to sustain the unsustainable and overcommit the organization to institutionalization. As a result, some management processes must also be flexible and appropriately fast. Flexible and fast management processes keep the organization on its toes and prevent rigidity from setting in. They help companies string together momentary competitive advantages that sustain high performance.

Designing Good Management Processes

Good management processes align resources to the strategy and apply the "plan, do, check, act" logic of continuous improvement popularized by quality guru W. Edwards Deming.[7] These systems should focus attention and resources on the economic logic of the company and channel resources to its most important activities. Many organizations fail to do these basics well or consistently. In addition, organizations often fail the "check" step by making invalid assumptions regarding performance or skipping over the "check" step entirely. While good management processes are a necessary condition for survival, they are not sufficient.

Among the companies in our research that performed the management basics exceptionally well were the Brioche Pasquier Group, a multinational bakery headquartered in Les Cerqueux, France, and Netflix Inc., based in Los Gatos, California, which streams digital content to more than 100 million customers in more than 190 countries.

Brioche Pasquier This company relies heavily on a rolling three-year strategic plan that it develops with broad participation from the field and that provides the basis for its six-month planning and operations cycle. Each production and sales facility has profit-and-loss responsibility for its local market, and the company's priority action plans contain a set of initiatives focused on enhancing current and future results. If, for example, the three-year plan highlights the importance of developing a more sophisticated sales and business development capability to capture future market share, site-level plans may address sales capability development as well.

The priority action plan also contains initiatives from a bottom-up process. Every six months, managers facilitate a two- to three-hour "mini-diagnosis" with their teams. They encourage employees to identify the difficulties, defects, and dysfunctions encountered in their work and propose improvement initiatives. Although most initiatives are local, enterprise-wide changes can also be suggested. A coordination seminar among production managers and the key functional staff validate the site's priority action plan. All this happens in a couple of weeks.

The aligned initiatives and projects are codified into individual or team-based improvement plans that focus on improving current performance or how "slack resources" can be used to try out new ideas (for example, new kinds of in-store demos) to drive future success.

Over time, the improvement plans have essentially replaced job descriptions. Twice a year, individuals and teams identify objectives and actions related to their work that they think can improve short-term performance or develop future capability, and also do a review of the previous plans. Brioche Pasquier uses this as an opportunity to distribute monetary bonuses (funded by savings or new value realized) to the individuals and teams whose actions contributed to the results.

Netflix Netflix management sums up its overall corporate philosophy with the phrase "freedom & responsibility." The company wants every manager to be a leader, never settles for a mediocre hire, pays high salaries, and gives managers tremendous latitude rather than lots of rules to follow. Reflecting this philosophy, the planning and goal-alignment process begins with a quarterly business review. Everyone leaves the meeting with a clear understanding of key issues: what's important, what is and *isn't* working, next steps, and how the organization will approach growth for every product and market. That information is available to anyone in the organization.

Netflix doesn't draw a distinction between being a good leader and being a good manager. Planning, leading, and holding people accountable at Netflix are part of an organizational capacity to get the right stuff done. It is a system. Leading people is not a function of one's position in the hierarchy or an individual trait to be taught to those identified as "high potentials." There is

Everyone gives and gets feedback — from team members, supervisors, managers, and customers. There is a shared belief at Netflix that good results depend on people weighing in with their perspectives.

an expectation that anyone can take initiative, make decisions, and influence others in line with the company's strategy. Everyone gives and gets feedback—from team members, supervisors, managers, and customers. There is a shared belief at Netflix that good results depend on people weighing in with their perspectives. It's part of an overall system that stresses transparency. Getting alignment on direction and getting results the right way are critical. People who fail to achieve these are asked to leave the company.

We found that having the fundamentals right—having well-designed and well-executed management processes—is only a prerequisite for agility. Sustaining high performance was a function of whether certain processes were flexible and fast.

Designing Agile Management Processes

Good management processes support strategy and capability execution; *agile* management processes help to change capabilities and other organization features quickly when change is necessary. Brioche Pasquier, for instance, has transitioned from a single brioche plant and one local market to multiple factories, products, and production technologies. Along the way, it has learned to orchestrate complex international supply chains and adapt its capabilities to a multinational environment. These transformations were facilitated by the way the management processes were designed. Netflix, meanwhile, has shifted its strategic capabilities at least three times since its founding—from distributing DVDs to movie streaming, from negotiating for distribution rights to creating and developing its own content, and from piggybacking on server farms owned by third parties to building and operating its own content delivery network.

Netflix is currently learning to operate through international regulations as a global business.

An important point is that not *all* management processes need to be designed for flexibility and speed. Some, such as those governing the manufacturing and delivery processes at Brioche Pasquier and the core business at Netflix, just need to be extremely reliable and incorporate continuous improvement tools such as Six Sigma. However, for the management processes that are central to adaptation, such as resource allocation, performance management, and new product development, speed and flexibility are critical to ensure that new strategies and capabilities can be implemented seamlessly.

Increasing Flexibility and Speed

One essential aspect of agile management processes is flexibility—the ability to operate effectively without being tied to a rigid set of steps. Thus, flexible management processes are different from simple process improvements. Flexibility requires having a clear understanding of what the management process is supposed to achieve, functional links to a portfolio of inputs, and the freedom to adapt the process as necessary. While the purpose of the process must be well established and widely shared, the information needed by the process and the means to the ends shouldn't be fixed or narrow.

For example, most people agree that the purpose of goal setting is to ensure individual and team alignment to strategies and objectives. However, just aligning top-down objectives is not adequate. In addition to coming from management, goals can come from customer requests, compliance mandates, internal customer

Making Management Processes Flexible and Fast
Well-designed management processes help a company execute its
strategy and exercise its capabilities. Agile management processes go
a step further: They help the organization change when needed.

Well-Designed Management Processes	Agile Management Processes	
	Flexible Management Processes	Fast Management Processes
• Align resources/ behaviors to business strategy • Follow a continuous improvement "plan-do-check-act" logic • Support and align with other management processes	• Align tightly around the process' purpose and outcomes • Focus on effectiveness more than efficiency; how the process is conducted can vary • Accept a wide variety of inputs	• Have cycle times adjusted to fit the rhythm of the market • Consist of simple, not overly complex, processes that are easily explained • Involve wide sharing of relevant information and transparency

requirements, or be based on personal development objectives.
How to achieve alignment, then, should not be overly specific.

The priority action plan process at Brioche Pasquier is flexible
because the goal of developing a clear and shared plan is widely
understood and has two primary inputs: a top-down source in
the form of a strategic plan, and a bottom-up source in the form
of the mini-diagnoses at the team level. It is based on a changing
portfolio of objectives and strategies that are reviewed annually
at the company level. Knowing that the company's long-term
direction is always under review sends a powerful message that
nothing is permanent. At the plant level, input from the workforce about what is not working and what needs fixing helps set
the agenda for what types of future investments are needed.

Without flexibility, employees will focus on goals and budgets that are outdated rather than doing the right things at the right time. Speed is also enabled by simplicity and transparency.

Netflix's planning process is similar to Brioche Pasquier's in that business reviews send objectives down the organization so people pay close attention to strategy alignment. The company's leadership philosophy gives managers wide latitude to innovate in ways that are consistent with their job function, the product they are supporting, and the market. Netflix's freedom and responsibility framework[8] ensures a portfolio of inputs, gets alignment without overspecifying behaviors, and encourages effectiveness and variety over standardization.

Agile management processes are also appropriately fast. Agile organizations match process cycle times to the pace of environmental and business change. Whereas traditional management processes revolve around commitments to performance targets for defined periods (for example, one year), agile companies resist tying management processes to fixed time frames that may not properly align with the pace of change.[9] The rationale is clear: Without flexibility, employees will focus on goals and budgets that are outdated rather than doing the right things at the right time. Speed is also enabled by simplicity and transparency.

Rather than using a conventional annual cycle, Brioche Pasquier's easily explained priority action plan is tied to a semi-annual cycle. Executives share information and their thinking about the company every six months, and they interact with employees and managers in a variety of planning, strategizing, and operating processes. There is very little that is not widely known at Brioche Pasquier. Netflix, for its part, has found that, given the rapid pace and the level of uncertainty in its business, a quarterly focus is appropriate. Netflix executives are committed to putting information into the hands of the people who do the work and making sure that the information flows up and down to everyone who needs it.

Executives are committed to putting information into the hands of the people who do the work and making sure that the information flows up and down to everyone who needs it.

Pursuing innovative organizational structures, breaking the rules, and challenging the fundamentals of managing and leading make for great headlines, but they cannot create an effective and adaptable organization unless the basics are already in place. Agile organizations aren't created overnight. They require patient and committed leaders who attend to how the various organizational systems—including management processes—work together. In every organization we studied—even the ones that displayed high levels of agility—managers said the same thing: "There's still so much we need to learn." Alignment, another classic management principle, will be as relevant in the future as it is today.

11

Building the Right Ecosystem for Innovation

Nathan Furr and Andrew Shipilov

When markets become disrupted by new technologies and competitors, many legacy companies struggle to keep up. They are often simply ill-prepared to develop new products and services in the midst of the uncertainty. Rather than attempting to go it alone in such circumstances, some companies reach out to partners with an eye toward building a broader ecosystem that will boost their competitive strength. But what types of ecosystems will work best in a dynamic environment?

Perhaps the most common forms of ecosystems are centralized, where the company functions as the "hub." These tend to work well in stable environments where the key issues have already been worked out. In Amazon.com Inc.'s ecosystem for e-books, for example, the online retailer works with the maker of its Kindle tablets and an array of book publishers but keeps the respective partners separate from one another.

However, in many settings today, the requirements are fluid and the objectives less defined. What's needed, therefore, isn't a broker or intermediary to link the various partners but an *orchestrator* who can find connections among different partners and encourage them to work directly with one another to identify new or nascent opportunities. Rather than building a centralized ecosystem, the orchestrator's job is to create what we call an adaptive ecosystem, where partners develop significant projects or innovations together.[1] For companies, this requires both imagination and flexibility.

Driving Innovation

In our most recent research on how organizations generate value from their corporate alliances and partnerships, we've studied how certain companies, including Samsung, Mastercard, Lowe's, and Cisco Systems, have used adaptive ecosystems to define new offerings. Unlike traditional, centralized ecosystems, which tend to rely on partners that have fairly obvious tie-ins to the existing business model (as Amazon had with the Kindle maker and book publishers), companies using adaptive ecosystems frequently work with partners with less conventional capabilities.[2] For this reason, we refer to them as "uncommon partners."

Samsung Electronics Co. Ltd.'s recent experience developing a personal health–monitoring business offers a good example. In the past, the company's innovation efforts were geared toward being a fast follower as opposed to a market leader. To support its goals, Samsung coordinated innovation activities centrally through its strategy and innovation center. But as the company evaluated opportunities in personal health monitoring, it reached out to more than 20 startups and academic researchers working in fields related to blood pressure, hydration, and nutrition. In addition, it developed a close working relationship with Nestlé S.A., the Swiss food conglomerate. Although Nestlé had no experience in consumer electronics, it had done significant research on the impact of nutrition on the human body.

Centralized versus Adaptive Ecosystem Strategies
How, why, and when different strategies work.

	Centralized Ecosystem	Adaptive Ecosystem
Structure	A "broker" company connects to partners but keeps them separate, forcing them to work through itself.	An "orchestrator" company connects multiple partners and encourages them to work directly with one another.
Partners	The partners are familiar complements to the company's existing business model.	The company seeks out unfamiliar partners with different business models.
Why it's used	Partners are coordinated by the broker company to capture value (primarily for the broker).	Partners are encouraged to combine their diverse resources to create value (for all companies) quickly, flexibly, and at low cost.
When to use it	When industry boundaries are stable.	When industry boundaries are shifting.
Strategic focus	Start with a specific problem (such as how to sell e-books online).	Start with a "battlefield"—an area you want to explore (such as how to use blockchain or AI technologies in your business).
Relationships	Maintain arm's-length relationships and attract partners via traditional outreach methods.	Forge cooperative and supportive relationships and attract new partners with "bat signals."
Impact on the focal company	The broker changes in a limited way because its business model is stable.	The orchestrator transforms from the "inside out" as it learns from partners and changes its business model.

Assembling a network of other outside partners, Samsung
then set out to develop a platform (which it calls "The Voice of
the Body") where users and their doctors can monitor health
and medical issues using the latest technology. In contrast to
how things work in a centralized hub ecosystem (where each
partner coordinates separately with the company), the partners
work as a team to create new tools for improving medical care.
Eventually, Samsung envisions introducing devices capable of
collecting users' biological data and interpreting it in real time,
refining the results using algorithms based on an elaborate user
database. Although Samsung's focus is electronics, the opportunities could extend beyond monitoring devices. The company
also sees possibilities for developing food products that have
clinically proven health benefits.

In adaptive ecosystems, it can be difficult to predict all of
the required expertise and capabilities. As opportunities arise,
orchestrators need to be prepared to revisit the mix of partners.
The payment processing industry, which is undergoing tremendous change, provides a case in point. Over the years, Mastercard
International Inc. has competed against Visa Inc. and American
Express Co. with a centralized ecosystem strategy in which it
interacts seamlessly with a long list of banks and merchants
that use Mastercard's infrastructure to process payments from
its customers. More recently, however, Mastercard saw opportunities to broaden its scope of business. Rather than restrict itself
to credit cards, the company wanted to develop new offerings
in the growing realm of digital payments. To do this, it needed
an adaptive ecosystem that could develop new offerings tai-
lored to emerging consumer needs. In London, for example,
it began working with Transport for London (the authority in
charge of the city's subway, train, and bus transportation), Cubic

Transportation Systems (the transit infrastructure provider), and retailers in the consumer goods business.

So far, Mastercard's efforts to move into new areas with new partners have been encouraging. Since payment solutions can be easily embedded in smartphones, configuring Mastercard's payment platform to pay for train and bus use is a no-brainer. But by working with partners and using both historical data about commuter behavior and a steady stream of new data, Mastercard is also hoping to drive improvements in the commuting experience. For example, in an effort to shift ridership away from the busiest periods of the day, it could offer commuters discounts at coffee shops and other businesses if they opted not to use transportation systems during certain times of day. Mastercard executives we interviewed suggested that relatively small changes in consumer behavior—as little as a few minutes at the right times—could make a big difference. Indeed, for every 1% shift in peak demand, large cities such as London, Chicago, or New York City might save millions of dollars in delayed capital expenditures each year and, more important, create a more pleasant experience for travelers.

Implementing an Adaptive Ecosystem Strategy

How does a company implement an adaptive ecosystem strategy? Based on our research, we have identified a series of essential activities.

Define the "Battlefield"

While centralized ecosystem strategies depend on having specific, well-defined problems and solutions (how to sell e-books online or how to equip houses with solar panels, for example), adaptive ecosystem strategies are suited for situations where the problem and the solution are uncertain or still being sorted out.

As a result, you need to start by defining the "battlefield"—or the area to explore. From there, you can begin to assemble an ecosystem to explore the challenge and refine it as your understanding about the opportunity evolves. Mastercard, for example, wanted to learn how it could use artificial intelligence (AI) in its business. To understand how AI could be integrated with payment solutions, it reached out to Pizza Hut LLC and SoftBank Corp., a Japanese telecommunications and internet company that has investments in a number of technology startups.

Working together, the companies developed a new mobile customer interface using Pepper, SoftBank's humanoid robot, as a diner's assistant in some Pizza Hut restaurants. The robot identifies customers from their mobile phones, recommends the day's specials, and takes orders. Mastercard's technology allows customers to pair their phones with the robot for identification purposes and to process transactions. The robot, in effect, assumes the role of cashier and lightens the load for servers. For Mastercard, this move into robotics represents a radical step.

Use "Bat Signals" to Attract Partners

After defining the battlefield, orchestrators need to find and attract the right partners. In our experience, some of the most successful adaptive ecosystem strategies have been achieved when companies were able to connect with uncommon partners on the outer fringes of their industries—or even beyond the traditional boundaries of their industries. However, identifying the capabilities required for innovation can be challenging: You don't know precisely what you will need along the journey, and you simply don't know what you don't know.

Orchestrators need to be willing to experiment with new ways of doing things. Consider this example: Lowe's Companies Inc., a home improvement retail chain based in North Wilkesboro, North Carolina, wanted to explore opportunities in the emerging 3-D printing and additive manufacturing business. So, it reached out to a range of potential partners already in that market, including a developer of 3-D designs, a provider of high-volume distributed 3-D printing, an industrial 3-D printing company, a design agency, and a sensor manufacturer. Kyle Nel, founder of Lowe's Innovation Labs, described this part of the process as putting out "bat signals," in hopes that the right set of partners would come together. Management recognized that moving away from the company's established retail business and into a new market would be challenging and require a new business model—one flexible enough to enable customers to design things they could print from stores. The partners Lowe's recruited to the new ecosystem brought not only the capabilities necessary to enable the new business venture, but also key insights about how to attract customers to the offering. To promote the new capability, Lowe's designed a media campaign and released a series of videos, which in turn have attracted some additional new partners.

Eager to develop new ideas for growing its overall business, Cisco Systems Inc., the technology multinational company based in San Jose, California, is taking a similar approach. It has released a series of videos describing initiatives it has explored in conjunction with other companies through CHILL (Cisco Hyperinnovation Living Labs)—undertakings that Cisco says likely would have been too difficult, too expensive, or too intangible to pursue on its own.[3] In the area of health care, for example, Cisco recently brought together senior executives from drugstore chain Walgreens, enterprise software company Vocera

Communications, the University of California at San Francisco, and other organizations for a two-day meeting. Participants worked as an adaptive ecosystem on new initiatives such as virtual care and connected hospitals. Cisco has since launched CHILL-X startups made up of companies cofounded by the ecosystem and piloted by an experienced CEO.

For its part, Samsung has taken a slightly more conservative approach. It organizes networking events to which it invites potential partners (including competitors) and experts from different disciplines. Recently, for example, it brought people together to discuss topics including medical imaging, solar-enabled transportation solutions, pediatrics, and AI. Samsung uses the conferences to gauge which partners are most valuable and then initiates discussions with them.

Connect Uncommon Partners

While centralized ecosystems are frequently based on arm's-length transactions that keep partners separate from one another, adaptive ecosystems are structured to encourage cross-fertilization. Their effectiveness depends on close and supportive collaborations between the organizing company and the partners, and also *among* the partners. Moreover, adaptive ecosystems perform best when made up of partners from outside one another's traditional ecosystems. Having uncommon partners helps the company at the center explore unfamiliar terrain.

Making this happen can be challenging because most of the partners may have never worked with one another and there are few models for such collaboration. Cisco's recent work with companies including global logistics company DHL, construction equipment manufacturer Caterpillar, and aeronautical company Airbus to create a new digital supply chain provides a useful example. In 2015, Cisco brought more than 80 people together in Berlin for a brainstorming session to think of ways in which manufacturers could manage global inventory in a more flexible manner and better forecast problems with component supplies before they arise. The collaborators sought ways to enable companies to track shipments more precisely with sensors and authenticate the sources of components with blockchain technology. The possible uses of blockchain technology in supply chain management are wide-ranging. In the near term, companies will be able to use secure, digitized supply chains to monitor and authenticate specific spare airplane parts, for instance, or the origins of the diamonds used in jewelry. Such breakthroughs would not have been possible without an ecosystem of uncommon partners.

Companies with experience in adaptive ecosystems are finding that, by definition, collaborations don't follow a set pattern. Thus, Cisco has found advantages in working with a core group of partners across multiple projects. According to Kate O'Keeffe, senior director of Cisco's CHILL initiative, such stability allows people on both sides to gain critical experience they can apply to other projects.

Glue the Partners Together
Centralized and adaptive ecosystems have one important thing in common: Orchestrators provide the "glue" that gives the ecosystem its infrastructure and holds it in place. For Lowe's, the glue for the adaptive ecosystem is the network of physical stores and the direct connection to customers that those stores provide. For Samsung, it's the ability to manufacture or distribute electronics on a massive scale. In Amazon's Kindle initiative, the glue for the centralized ecosystem is the online retailer's

distribution power, tablet design, and digital rights management software. A well-recognized brand can also act as glue.

But adaptive ecosystems give companies opportunities to develop new forms of glue that connect multiple partners to one another and become the ecosystem's distinctive source of value. For example, in Samsung's health information project, the glue is the hardware and software that integrate the sensors and analytics to create an individualized and dynamic picture of a person's health. For Mastercard, the glue will be the advanced technologies its ecosystem deploys to securely identify users— technologies that could also be applied to government ID systems and secure interfaces for robots and cars. In fact, through our interviews with Mastercard, we learned that the company is collaborating with General Motors Co. on solutions that will enable smartphones equipped with proprietary software to unlock a car, start the engine, and otherwise interact with the vehicle.

Leverage Opportunities to Transform from the Inside Out

Not all adaptive ecosystem efforts will lead to successful innovations or market entries. As with any business strategy, there are risks. Still, adaptive ecosystems provide companies with opportunities to transform the way they do business. Many executives participating in adaptive ecosystems emphasize the importance of learning from companies that are accustomed to operating in different markets. For example, Groupe Galeries Lafayette, an upscale French retailer, created a startup accelerator whose aim is to disrupt its traditional brick-and-mortar business. In the accelerator, several startups have begun to work together to create digital solutions to enhance the retail experience. Philippe Houzé, the company's executive chairman, told us that building the ecosystem of startups has been key to helping Galeries Lafayette transform the "inside from the outside." Previously, Houzé explained, senior executives often resisted changes to the business model, but exposure to the startups has made them more flexible.[4]

The transformation occurs because, by sharing information and ideas with partners from other spheres, companies can extend their sense of what's possible—in their markets and in their organizations. Recently, Mastercard has been using its adaptive ecosystem strategy to identify new growth opportunities. One area it is exploring is the internet of things, which has led to an emerging partnership with Samsung. The two companies, now both adept at managing adaptive ecosystems, are collaborating to create a smart refrigerator that can monitor the supply levels of everyday items, place orders, and arrange for payment and delivery. Depending on the user's settings, the refrigerator could analyze families' purchasing habits and make suggestions for their shopping lists.

Mastercard is continuing to look for other ways to work with partners in extending its digital platforms into new markets. In January 2017, it began working with farming enterprise Producers Direct, based in Nairobi, Kenya, and London, and the Bill and Melinda Gates Foundation on a pilot program called 2KUZE that will build a platform to enable small farmers in Kenya and other East African countries to sell their crops to wholesale customers and receive fairer and secure payments. Few of the farmers have bank accounts, but most have mobile phones, so the platform will allow them to receive payments directly through their phones. Mastercard says it wants to apply what it learns on this project to markets in the developed world.

Make Contracts Flexible

When you're building an adaptive ecosystem that will venture into uncertain technologies, it is impossible to write partnership agreements that spell out every possible contingency. Thus, many adaptive ecosystems don't start with onerous contracts detailing precise deliverables or distribution of value. Instead, companies use simple framework agreements that emphasize the general boundaries of cooperation and leave a lot of room for adapting to specific technological discoveries and new business models as they take shape.

Ecosystems need to align with an industry's life cycle. Adaptive ecosystems are best suited to emerging industries where there are significant uncertainties and the broader environment is not yet well defined. Centralized ecosystems work for mature industries and stable contexts. Over time, a company's ecosystem strategy will evolve: As industries that were once unsettled begin to mature and the value-creation patterns become more established, companies may move toward favoring centralized management over adaptive models. How this pattern plays out will vary from ecosystem to ecosystem.

More significantly, companies engaging in ecosystem strategies are building collaboration and network muscles that will serve them well over their entire life spans. Indeed, the ability to discover and leverage new forms of value in collaboration with unexpected partners is likely to extend a company's life span. Organizations with the ability to flex with, read, and react to market shifts with an evolving set of collaborators are well suited to a competitive environment whose twists and turns have no end in sight.

12

Implement First, Ask Questions Later (or Not at All)

Stephen J. Andriole

Facebook Inc. founder Mark Zuckerberg nicely summarized a modern philosophy about technology innovation when he spoke about the need to "move fast and break things." Increasingly, that same mindset appears to drive how companies implement new technologies as well. And this phenomenon stretches beyond Silicon Valley.

For decades, companies required their information technology (IT) teams to identify, model, and validate business requirements before writing a line of code or adopting a new technology platform, product, or service. Today, that approach seems almost quaint. Companies no longer build giant flowcharts, analyze tasks, or model business requirements in advance of deploying new technology. They just pilot and adopt—often before they have a clear idea of the business problem they're trying to solve. Once, this launch-first mentality would have been considered heresy. Yet it has become the norm, driven by the accelerating pace of technology change, the fear of losing market share to disruptive new players, and the ease with which new technologies can be implemented through cloud-based delivery. This is a challenging environment, particularly for tradition-bound organizations. But it's the new reality and CIOs must adapt, or they risk permanently falling behind the competition.

As part of a larger study on changes in technology implementation, my team spent two years collecting survey and interview data about the evolving relationship between business and technology. We talked to people in business roles and technology roles at companies across a range of industries. The most significant finding was the rapid death of detailed requirements analysis and modeling. Among survey respondents, 71% believed that technology can be deployed without a specific problem in mind. Just one-third said they have a clearly defined process for the adoption of emerging technology. Perhaps most surprising, half of the respondents described their pilot initiatives—small-scale, low-cost rapid testing of new technology—as "purely experimental," with no requirements analysis at all.

We heard a consistent theme. As one business process manager at a Fortune 100 pharmaceutical company put it, "We've abandoned the strict 'requirements-first, technology-second' adoption process, whatever that really means. Why? Because we want to stay agile and competitive and want to leverage new technologies. Gathering requirements takes forever and hasn't made our past projects more successful."

Different Software, Different Approach

The very idea that technologies would be acquired and deployed without documented, validated requirements flies in the face of what technology and business professionals were taught for decades in the 20th century. It was often the business side that insisted upon elaborate requirements gathering and validation. Executives frequently complained about the rush to deploy untested technologies or—worse—technologies with unverified total-cost-of-ownership (TCO) or return-on-investment (ROI) models.

Today's adoption models assume that emerging new technologies drive requirements, not the other way around—which is why many tech solutions get discovered as part of the implementation process rather than in advance of it. Said a little differently, many companies have no clear idea what they will do with specific technologies but believe that there's huge potential in the technology that will become clear over time, and that they have no choice but to quickly adopt emerging technology if they want to digitally transform their companies to remain competitive.

This approach is possible because of the way software itself has changed. Rather than massive, enterprise-wide systems that cost millions and take years to implement, software today is cloud-based and relatively inexpensive. It often addresses highly specific problems, sometimes limited to a single business unit or department. And technology is evolving continually. As a result, companies feel they need to move fast, try a lot of things, and accept the inevitable failures. If something doesn't work, the stakes are a lot lower—costs are measured in tens of thousands of dollars rather than millions, and timelines are a few months rather than a few years.

"We've piloted new devices and applications—especially mobile applications—at a quick pace," the technology manager at an insurance company told us. "The good news is that failures happen fast and are usually cheap because of cloud delivery. The cloud changes the way we think about pilots. It makes it easy for us to 'fail fast and fail cheap'—something everyone likes, especially the CFO."

This approach isn't 100% new, of course. So-called shadow IT—in which business units go rogue and create their own work-arounds, implementing technology without the knowledge or permission of the CIO—has long plagued many companies. In the past, those efforts could have major ramifications, breaking security protocols and contaminating data sets. Today, shadow IT has essentially won. Technology at many companies is now highly decentralized—it happens at the level of individual business units, and the heads of those units have wide latitude to launch pilot tests when they spot something that might work.

As we heard from the business unit vice president at a media company, "Shadow IT short-circuits requirements analysis—which isn't all bad, right? The business units will do what they need to do to make money, and sometimes that means they'll adopt technology immediately if they think it might solve some problems. . . . There's no way I can shut it down even if I wanted to, which I don't."

Little Analysis of Pilot Tests

Perhaps the most surprising finding from our analysis was that most of the companies piloting new technologies fail to quantitatively measure the impact of the pilots in terms of ROI or TCO. This is another major departure from best practices of the past, when companies had elaborate metrics in place to measure the returns on these investments. Today, the embrace of new technology can be driven by fear as much as a quest for improved performance. Companies are moving so fast that they don't have time to gauge results.

Indeed, when we asked survey participants about the factors behind rapid technology adoption, the answers were relatively consistent across industries.

Most of the companies piloting new technologies fail to quantitatively measure the impact of the pilots in terms of ROI or TCO.

Reducing costs was a big factor for companies, along with the opportunity to digitally transform themselves and roll out new business models. Yet competitive fear was the third most common factor. Companies face such a broad range of threats and disruptions, including new market entrants from a wide variety of directions, that they feel they have no choice but to jump into new technology headfirst.

Under this mindset, formal after-the-fact analyses of pilot tests miss the point, and there's little time for them anyway. Business leaders don't have the luxury of debriefing after a pilot to ask, "How well is this working?" If it works, they'll know. Besides, the thinking goes, the ROI just isn't as important when the "I"—the actual investment in new technology—is so low.

Notably, our findings show that the pressure to move fast in technology adoption is not coming from the C-suite or senior management but from business units closer to the action. The technology is changing so quickly—and affecting operational functions several layers below them in the org chart—that most senior leaders can't keep up with recent advances, let alone develop a strategic approach to their deployment.

New Best Practices

It would be hard to find a CIO from the 1990s who would have predicted the death of formal, validated business requirements and the rise of a technology-first adoption process. Even today, this philosophy will undoubtedly anger and confuse traditional corporate budgeteers who crave precision. But we live in a different world in which speed matters more than precision, and there's no going back.

In this world, the new best practices are to move fast, adopt early, and experiment widely. Companies should identify a

The Drivers of Rapid Technology Adoption

Across industries, there is a broad consensus that the opportunities to reduce costs and digitally transform are the biggest factors behind the shift to more rapid implementation, followed by competitive fear.

Industry (group)	Opportunities to reduce costs	Opportunities for digital transformation	Competitive fear	Consumer product awareness (for example, iPads)	Pressure from the business units	Pressure from the C-suite	Pressure from senior management	Pressure from line management
Automotive	50%	100%	50%	0%	0%	0%	0%	0%
Banking	50%	33%	67%	0%	17%	17%	0%	0%
Consulting	43%	29%	29%	57%	43%	29%	43%	0%
Consumer	100%	100%	100%	50%	0%	0%	0%	0%
Education	44%	67%	22%	33%	33%	22%	11%	11%
Energy	80%	80%	20%	40%	20%	0%	0%	0%
Engineering	80%	20%	80%	0%	0%	0%	0%	0%
Financial Services	63%	69%	50%	38%	38%	25%	19%	6%
Food and Beverage	100%	33%	0%	67%	67%	33%	0%	67%
Government	83%	100%	33%	67%	0%	0%	0%	0%
Health Care	77%	46%	54%	38%	46%	31%	31%	8%
Insurance	33%	67%	67%	33%	33%	33%	0%	0%
Manufacturing	40%	40%	40%	60%	60%	0%	20%	20%
Media	100%	100%	50%	50%	50%	50%	50%	50%
Pharmaceuticals	80%	40%	60%	40%	60%	20%	40%	0%
Retail	100%	50%	0%	0%	0%	50%	0%	0%
Technology Services	71%	79%	71%	57%	36%	21%	21%	7%
Telecommunications	50%	25%	50%	25%	25%	13%	13%	13%
Transportation	100%	50%	0%	50%	50%	0%	0%	0%

specific transformation target, like supply chain planning, manufacturing operations, or customer relationship management. They should also select a few technologies, such as analytics, artificial intelligence, or location-based services. And then they should start launching pilot tests to see what works, with the goal of rapidly scaling up winning initiatives.

Business requirements may literally be unknowable until companies can try out the new technologies, and many of those pilots will fail. But the alternative—trying to move slowly and deliberately, with business requirements clearly spelled out in advance—is no longer an option. Companies should expect to discover solutions through the implementation process rather than in advance of it. They'll break things, undoubtedly. But they'll also stay ahead of the competition.

Contributors

Stephen J. Andriole is the Thomas G. Labrecque Professor of Business Technology at the Villanova School of Business in Villanova, Pennsylvania.

Jacques Bughin is a senior partner in the Brussels office of the management consulting firm McKinsey & Co. as well as a director of the McKinsey Global Institute.

Thomas H. Davenport is the President's Distinguished Professor of IT and Management at Babson College in Wellesley, Massachusetts; a fellow at the MIT Initiative on the Digital Economy and at NewVantage Partners; and a senior adviser to Deloitte Analytics. He is the author of *The AI Advantage* (MIT Press, 2018) and other books.

Nathan Furr is an assistant professor of strategy at INSEAD in Fontainebleau, France.

Lynn J. Good is the CEO of Duke Energy in Charlotte, North Carolina.

David Kiron is the executive editor of *MIT Sloan Management Review*.

Edward E. Lawler III is the Distinguished Professor of Business and director of the Center for Effective Organizations at the University of Southern California in Los Angeles. He is a coauthor of *The Agility Factor* (Jossey-Bass, 2014).

Vikram Mahidhar is the head of AI business at Genpact, a professional services firm focused on delivering digital transformation based in New York.

Paul Michelman is the editor in chief of *MIT Sloan Management Review*.

Jeanne Ross is a principal research scientist for MIT's Center for Information Systems Research.

Paul J. H. Schoemaker is the former research director of the Mack Center for Technological Innovation at the University of Pennsylvania's Wharton School and the coauthor, with Steven Krupp, of *Winning the Long Game: How Strategic Leaders Shape the Future* (PublicAffairs, 2014).

Andrew Shipilov is a professor of strategy and the John H. Loudon Chair of International Management at INSEAD in Fontainebleau, France.

Charles Sull is a partner at Charles Thames Strategy Partners LLC.

Donald Sull is a senior lecturer at the MIT Sloan School of Management.

Philip E. Tetlock is the Annenberg University Professor at the University of Pennsylvania and coauthor, with Dan Gardner, of *Superforecasting: The Art and Science of Prediction* (Crown, 2015).

Stefano Turconi is a teaching fellow at the London Business School.

Nicolas van Zeebroeck is a professor of innovation and digital business at the Solvay Brussels School of Economics and Management at Université libre de Bruxelles in Brussels.

Peter Weill is a senior research scientist and the chair of MIT Sloan School of Management's Center for Information Systems Research.

Thomas Williams is an independent management consultant based in Ridgway, Colorado.

Stephanie L. Woerner is a research scientist at the MIT Sloan School of Management's Center for Information Systems Research.

Christopher G. Worley is a professor of strategy and entrepreneurship at NEOMA Business School in Reims, France.

James Yoder is a former chief data scientist at Charles Thames Strategy Partners LLC.

Notes

Chapter 2

1. In the MIT CISR 2015 CIO Digital Disruption Survey, we surveyed 413 enterprises. In the MIT CISR 2017 Pathways to Digital Business Transformation Survey, we surveyed 400 enterprises.

2. J. W. Ross, I. M. Sebastian, and C. M. Beath, "Digital Design: It's a Journey," research briefing, MIT CISR, April 21, 2016, https://cisr.mit .edu/blog/documents/2016/04/21/2016_0401_digitaldesign_rosssebastian beath.pdf.

3. J. W. Ross, P. Weill, and D. C. Robertson, *Enterprise Architecture as Strategy: Creating a Foundation for Business Execution* (Boston: Harvard Business Publishing, 2006), chaps. 1 and 2.

4. Our sources are company interviews and documents used with permission; Danske Bank's website, http://www.danskebank.com; and the MIT CISR 2012 IT Investment Survey, sample size of 354, developed countries only.

5. V. Vig Nielsen, "Danske Bank: A Winner in Digitalization," February 1, 2017, https://digit.hbs.org/submission/danske-bank-a-winner-in-digital ization/.

6. N. O. Fonstad, S. L. Woerner, and P. Weill, "mBank: Creating the Digital," research briefing, MIT CISR, October 15, 2015, https://cisr.mit .edu/blog/documents/2015/10/15/2015_1001_mbank_fonstadwoerner weill.pdf.

7. "Francisco González: 'We Are Building the Best Digital Bank of the 21st Century,'" BBVA, March 13, 2015, https://www.bbva.com/en/francisco -gonzalez-we-are-building-the-best-digital-bank-of-the-21st-century/.

8. Ross, Weill, and Robertson, *Enterprise Architecture as Strategy*, 61–64.

9. "Scotiabank to Buy ING Bank of Canada for \$3.1B," CBC, August 29, 2012, https://www.cbc.ca/news/business/scotiabank-to-buy-ing-bank-of -canada-for-3-1b-1.1160516/; "ING Direct to Become 'Capital One 360,' but Promises to Remain the Same," *Consumerist*, November 7, 2012, https://consumerist.com/2012/11/07/ing-direct-to-become-capital-one -360-but-promises-to-remain-the-same/; and "ING to Sell ING Direct UK to Barclays," press release, October 9, 2012, https://www.ing.com/Newsroom/ All-news/Press-releases/PROld/ING-to-sell-ING-Direct-UK-to-Barclays.htm.

10. "ING to Spend EUR800 Million on Digital Integration; Shed 7,000 Jobs," *Finextra*, October 3, 2016, https://www.finextra.com/newsarticle/ 29533/ing-to-spend-eur800-million-on-digital-integration-shed-7000 -jobs/; and "ING Strategy Update: Accelerating Think Forward," press release, October 3, 2016, https://www.ing.com/Newsroom/All-news /Press-releases/ING-strategy-update-Accelerating-Think-Forward.htm.

11. P. Weill and S. L. Woerner, "Becoming Better Prepared for Digital Disruption," *NACD Directorship Magazine*, March–April 2016, https:// www.nacdonline.org/insights/magazine/article.cfm?itemnumber=26118.

Chapter 3

1. M. E. Porter, "What Is Strategy?" *Harvard Business Review* 74, no. 6 (November–December 1996): 61–78.

2. D. Sull, *Why Good Companies Go Bad and How Great Managers Remake Them*, rev. ed. (Boston: Harvard Business Publishing, 2005).

3. See D. J. Collis and M. G. Rukstad, "Can You Say What Your Strategy Is?" *Harvard Business Review* 86, no. 4 (April 2008): 82–90; E. Van den Steen, "Formulating Strategy," Harvard Business School Teaching Note 714–485, March 2014; O. Gadiesh and J. L. Gilbert, "Transforming Corner-Office Strategy into Frontline Action," *Harvard Business Review* 79, no. 5 (May 2001): 72–79; and C. Markides, "Six Principles of Break-through Strategy," *Business Strategy Review* 10, no. 2 (1999): 1–10.

4. For a description of this research, see D. Sull and K. M. Eisenhardt, "Strategy as Simple Rules," in *Simple Rules: How to Thrive in a Complex World* (New York: Houghton Mifflin Harcourt, 2015).

5. The who/what/how framework was initially formulated by D. F. Abell in *Defining the Business: The Starting Point of Strategic Planning* (Englewood Cliffs, New Jersey: Prentice Hall, 1980) and refined and elaborated by Markides, "Six Principles of Breakthrough Strategy."

6. The strategy simplification approach deals with this problem by cramming many choices into a few overarching categories or omitting choices that will be crucial for some companies. A company's scope—one of three factors in the Collis and Rukstad (2008) framework—includes choices about target customers, product offering, geographic markets, and vertical integration.

7. For more details, see D. Sull and S. Turconi, "How to Recognize a Strategic Priority When You See One," *Strategic Agility Project* (blog), September 28, 2017, https://sloanreview.mit.edu/article/how-to-recognize -a-strategic-priority-when-you-see-one/.

8. For more details, see D. Sull and K. M. Eisenhardt, "Strategy as Simple Rules," in *Simple Rules: How to Thrive in a Complex World* (New York: Houghton Mifflin Harcourt, 2015).

9. N. Cowan, "The Magical Number 4 in Short-Term Memory: A Reconsideration of Mental Storage Capacity," *Behavioral and Brain Sciences* 24, no. 1 (February 2001): 87–114.

10. D. Sull, S. Turconi, and S. Zanjani, "Burberry's Digital Strategy," London Business School case study CS-15–007 (London: London Business School, 2016).

11. For a review of literature on factors contributing to corporate inertia, see Sull, *Why Good Companies Go Bad and How Great Managers Remake Them.*

12. W. Isaacson, *Steve Jobs* (New York: Simon & Schuster, 2011), 378.

13. For an early discussion, see C. von Clausewitz, *On War*, ed. and trans. M. E. Howard and P. Paret (Princeton, NJ: Princeton University Press, 1989), 623. For a recent and insightful discussion of complexity in battle, see US Marine Corps, *Warfighting* (Washington, DC: US Government Printing Office, 1997).

14. C. Perez Jr., ed., *Addressing the Fog of COG: Perspectives on the Center of Gravity in U.S. Military Doctrine* (Fort Leavenworth, Kansas: Combat Studies Institute Press, 2012).

15. Sample of 363 organizations that took the execution survey between 2012 and 2017.

16. To measure agreement on strategic priorities, we asked top team members to list their company's top three to five priorities over the next few years. We then grouped their free-text responses into categories of strategic priorities to create a matrix in which each row represents a manager and each column a strategic priority. We then calculated the five most frequently listed priorities, and calculated how many of the top team members listed at least three of the top five strategic priorities. For a fuller discussion of our methodology and robustness tests, see Sull and Turconi, "How to Recognize a Strategic Priority When You See One."

Chapter 6

1. M. Wenzel, D. Wagner, H.-T. Wagner, and J. Koch, "Digitization and Path Disruption: An Examination in the Funeral Industry," European Conference on Information Systems 2015 completed research papers, Paper 199, http://aisel.aisnet.org/ecis2015_cr/199/.

2. J. Bughin, L. LaBerge, and A. Mellbye, "The Case for Digital Reinvention," *McKinsey Quarterly*, February 2017, https://www.mckinsey.com/business-functions/digital-mckinsey/our-insights/the-case-for-digital-reinvention.

3. J. Bughin and N. van Zeebroeck, "The Case for Offensive Strategies in Response to Digital Disruption," iCite working paper number WP021–2017, Université libre de Bruxelles, Brussels, Belgium, April 2017, http://ftp.zew.de/pub/zew-docs/veranstaltungen/Presaentation.pdf.

4. L. Downes and P. Nunes, *Big Bang Disruption: Strategy in the Age of Devastating Innovation* (New York: Portfolio, 2014), 16–18.

5. W. Busch and J. P. Moreno, "Banks' New Competitors: Starbucks, Google, and Alibaba," *Harvard Business Review*, February 20, 2014, https://hbr.org/2014/02/banks-new-competitors-starbucks-google-and-alibaba/.

6. S. O'Hear, "Facebook Just Secured an E-Money License in Ireland, Paving the Way for Messenger Payments in Europe," *TechCrunch*, December 7, 2016, https://techcrunch.com/2016/12/07/facebook-just-secured-an-e-money-license-in-ireland-paving-way-for-messenger-payments-in-europe/.

7. The negative impact on incumbents increases as digitization spreads and deepens. This digital intensity factor was identified by Andrew

McAfee and Erik Brynjolfsson of MIT in 2008. See A. McAfee and E. Brynjolfsson, "Investing in the IT That Makes a Competitive Difference," *Harvard Business Review* 86, no. 7 (July–August 2008): 98–107.

8. A similarly named scientific hypothesis ("the Red Queen hypothesis") was put forth in 1973 by Leigh Van Valen to propose an explanation for biological evolution and extinction of species. The Red Queen concept was later applied to organizational strategy by William P. Barnett and Morten T. Hansen. See L. Van Valen, "A New Evolutionary Law," *Evolutionary Theory* 1 (1973): 1–30; and W. P. Barnett and M. T. Hansen, "The Red Queen in Organizational Evolution," *Strategic Management Journal* 17, no. S1 (Summer 1996): 139–157.

9. A. Dutta, H. Lee, and M. Yasai-Ardekani, "Digital Systems and Competitive Responsiveness: The Dynamics of IT Business Value," *Information & Management* 51, no. 6 (September 2014): 762–773.

10. D. Guilford, "BMW's DriveNow Is Profitable Now," *Automotive News*, October 3, 2016, http://www.autonews.com/article/20161003/GLOBAL/310039970/bmws-drivenow-is-profitable-now.

11. "Daimler, BMW Aim to Merge Their Carsharing Services: Manager Magazin," *Reuters*, December 15, 2016, https://www.reuters.com/article/us-germany-carsharing-daimler-bmw/daimler-bmw-aim-to-merge-their-carsharing-services-manager-magazin-idUSKBN144200/.

12. C. Bradley and C. O'Toole, "An Incumbent's Guide to Digital Disruption," *McKinsey Quarterly*, May 2016, https://www.mckinsey.com/business-functions/strategy-and-corporate-finance/our-insights/an-incumbents-guide-to-digital-disruption/.

13. B. Connolly, "CBA to Shake Up Payments with 'Albert' Launch," *CIO*, March 31, 2015, https://www.cio.com.au/article/571620/cba-shake-up-payments-albert-launch/.

Chapter 8

1. NewVantage, "Big Data Executive Survey 2018," January 2018, http://newvantage.com/wp-content/uploads/2018/01/Big-Data-Executive-Survey-2018-Findings.pdf.

2. Genpact and Fortune Knowledge Group, "Is Your Business AI-Ready?," 2017, http://www.genpact.com/lp/ai-research-c-suite/.

3. T. H. Davenport and R. Bean, "How Verizon Is Building a Big Data and AI Culture," *Forbes*, November 15, 2017, https://www.forbes.com/ sites/ciocentral/2017/11/15/how-verizon-is-building-a-big-data-and-ai -culture/.

4. T. H. Davenport and R. Bean, "How P&G and American Express Are Approaching AI," *Analytics* (blog), March 31, 2017, https://hbr.org/ 2017/03/how-pg-and-american-express-are-approaching-ai/.

5. T. Simonite, "Google's New Brain Could Have a Big Impact," *MIT Technology Review*, June 14, 2012, https://www.technologyreview.com/ s/428180/googles-new-brain-could-have-a-big-impact/.

6. J. Bresnick, "IBM Watson Becomes Unique Clinical Decision Support Tool," *Health IT Analytics*, October 22, 2014, https://healthitanalytics .com/news/ibm-watson-becomes-unique-clinical-decision-support-tool/.

7. T. H. Davenport and J. Kirby, "Just How Smart Are Smart Machines?" *MIT Sloan Management Review* 57, no. 3 (Spring 2016): 21–25.

8. Davenport and Kirby, "Just How Smart Are Smart Machines?"

9. T. H. Davenport, "What Data Scientist Shortage? Get Serious and Get Talent," *Data Informed*, May 17, 2016, http://data-informed.com/what -data-scientist-shortage-get-serious-and-get-talent/.

10. Z. Obermeyer and E. Emanuel, "Predicting the Future—Big Data, Machine Learning, and Clinical Medicine," New England Journal of Medicine 375 (2016): 1216–1219.

11. D. Hernandez, "Hospital Stumbles in Bid to Teach a Computer to Treat Cancer," *Wall Street Journal*, March 9, 2017, https://www.wsj.com/ articles/hospital-stumbles-in-bid-to-teach-a-computer-to-treat-cancer -1488969011.

Chapter 9

1. Two classic research anthologies are D. Kahneman, P. Slovic, and A. Tversky, eds., *Judgment under Uncertainty: Heuristics and Biases* (Cambridge: Cambridge University Press, 1982); and D. Kahneman and A. Tversky, eds., *Choices, Values, and Frames* (Cambridge: Cambridge University Press, 2000). See also W. M. Goldstein and R. M. Hogarth, eds., *Research on Judgment and Decision Making: Currents, Connections, and Controversies* (Cambridge: Cambridge University Press, 1997); D. J. Koehler and N. Harvey, eds., *Blackwell Handbook of Judgment and Decision*

Making (Malden, MA: Blackwell Publishing, 2004); and D. Kahneman, *Thinking, Fast and Slow* (New York: Farrar, Straus, and Giroux, 2011).

2. Readers can examine different probabilities of winning in tennis at "Tennis Calculator," 2015, http://www.mfbennett.com/cgi-bin/tennis calc.cgi. For analytical derivations, see F. J. G. M. Klaassen and J. R. Magnus, "Forecasting the Winner of a Tennis Match," *European Journal of Operational Research* 148, no. 2 (2003): 257–267.

3. E. Siegel, *Predictive Analytics: The Power to Predict Who Will Click, Buy, Lie, or Die* (Hoboken, NJ: John Wiley & Sons, 2013); and T. H. Davenport and J. G. Harris, *Competing on Analytics: The New Science of Winning* (Boston: Harvard Business Review Press, 2007).

4. K. Popper, "Of Clocks and Clouds," in *Learning, Development, and Culture: Essays in Evolutionary Epistemology*, ed. H. C. Plotkin (Hoboken, NJ: John Wiley & Sons, 1982), 109–119.

5. Notable books in this regard are J. Baron, *Thinking and Deciding*, 3rd ed. (Cambridge: Cambridge University Press, 2000); J. E. Russo and P. J. H. Schoemaker, *Winning Decisions: Getting It Right the First Time* (New York: Doubleday, 2001); G. Gigerenzer and R. Selten, eds., *Bounded Rationality: The Adaptive Toolbox* (Cambridge, MA: MIT Press, 2002); D. Ariely, *Predictably Irrational: The Hidden Forces That Shape Our Decisions* (New York: HarperCollins, 2008); and M. Lewis, *The Undoing Project* (New York: W. W. Norton, 2016).

6. P. E. Tetlock and D. Gardner, *Superforecasting: The Art and Science of Prediction* (New York: Crown, 2015).

7. P. J. H. Schoemaker and P. E. Tetlock, "Superforecasting: How to Upgrade Your Company's Judgment," *Harvard Business Review* 94, no. 5 (May 2016): 72–78.

8. For more details about best practices for setting up and running prediction tournaments, see Schoemaker and Tetlock, *Superforecasting*.

9. Prediction tournaments are scored using a rigorous, widely accepted yardstick known as the Brier score. For more information about the Brier score, see G. W. Brier, "Verification of Forecasts Expressed in Terms of Probability," *Monthly Weather Review* 78, no. 1 (January 1950): 1–3.

10. B. Fischhoff, "Debiasing," in *Judgment under Uncertainty*, ed. Kahneman, Slovic, and Tversky, 422–444; and J. S. Lerner and P. E. Tetlock, "Accounting for the Effects of Accountability," *Psychological Bulletin* 125, no. 2 (March 1999): 255–275.

11. B. Fischhoff, "Debiasing"; G. Keren, "Cognitive Aids and Debiasing Methods: Can Cognitive Pills Cure Cognitive Ills?," *Advances in Psychology* 68 (1990): 523–552; and H. R. Arkes, "Costs and Benefits of Judgment Errors: Implications for Debiasing," *Psychological Bulletin* 110, no. 3 (November 1991): 486–498.

12. The term "bootstrapping" has a different meaning in statistics, where it refers to repeated sampling from the same data set (with replacement) to get better estimates; see, for example, "Bootstrapping (Statistics)," Wikipedia, January 26, 2017, https://en.wikipedia.org/wiki/Bootstrapping_(statistics).

13. H. A. Wallace, "What Is in the Corn Judge's Mind?," *Journal of American Society for Agronomy* 15 (July 1923): 300–304.

14. S. Rose, "Improving Credit Evaluation," *American Banker*, March 13, 1990.

15. These tasks included, among others, predicting repayment of medical students' loans. See R. Cooter and J. B. Erdmann, "A Model for Predicting HEAL Repayment Patterns and Its Implications for Medical Student Finance," *Academic Medicine* 70, no. 12 (December 1995): 1134–1137. For more detail on how to build linear models—both objective and subjective—see A. H. Ashton, R. H. Ashton, and M. N. Davis, "White-Collar Robotics: Levering Managerial Decision Making," *California Management Review* 37, no. 1 (Fall 1994): 83–109. Especially useful is their discussion of possible objections to using linear models in applied settings, as in their example of predicting advertising space for *Time* magazine.

16. For a thorough analysis of the multiple reasons for this paradox, see C. F. Camerer and E. J. Johnson, "The Process-Performance Paradox in Expert Judgment: How Can Experts Know So Much and Predict So Badly?," chap. 10 in *Research on Judgment and Decision Making*, ed. Goldstein and Hogarth.

17. Random noise can produce much inconsistency within as well as across experts; see R. H. Ashton, "Cue Utilization and Expert Judgments: A Comparison of Independent Auditors with Other Judges," *Journal of Applied Psychology* 59, no. 4 (August 1974): 437–444; J. Shanteau, D. J. Weiss, R. P. Thomas, and J. C. Pounds, "Performance-Based Assessment of Expertise: How to Decide If Someone Is an Expert or Not," *European*

Journal of Operational Research 136, no. 2 (January 2002): 253–263; R. H. Ashton, "A Review and Analysis of Research on the Test-Retest Reliability of Professional Judgment," *Journal of Behavioral Decision Making* 13, no. 3 (July–September 2000): 277–294; S. Grimstad and M. Jørgensen, "Inconsistency of Expert Judgment-Based Estimates of Software Development Effort," *Journal of Systems and Software* 80, no. 11 (November 2007): 1770–1777; and A. Koriat, "Subjective Confidence in Perceptual Judgments: A Test of the Self-Consistency Model," *Journal of Experimental Psychology: General* 140, no. 1 (February 2011): 117–139.

18. Beyond just predictions, noise reduction is a broad strategy for improving decisions; see D. Kahneman, A. M. Rosenfield, L. Gandhi, and T. Blaser, "Noise: How to Overcome the High, Hidden Cost of Inconsistent Decision Making," *Harvard Business Review* 94, no. 10 (October 2016): 38–46.

19. The radiologist example was taken from P. J. Hoffman, P. Slovic, and L. G. Rorer, "An Analysis-of-Variance Model for Assessment of Configural Cue Utilization in Clinical Judgment," *Psychological Bulletin* 69, no. 5 (May 1968): 338–349. Note that these were highly trained professionals making judgments central to their work. In addition, they knew that their medical judgments were being examined by researchers, so they probably tried as hard as they could. Still, their carefully considered judgments were remarkably inconsistent.

20. The average intra-expert correlation was 0.76, which equates to a 23% chance of getting a reversal in the ranking or scores of two cases from one time to the next. In general, a Pearson product-moment correlation of r translates into a $[0.5 + \arcsin(r)/\pi]$ probability of a rank reversal of two cases the second time, assuming bivariate normal distributions; see M. Kendall, *Rank Correlation Methods* (London: Charles Griffen & Co., 1948).

21. A provocative brief for this structured numerical approach in medicine can be found in J. A. Swets, R. M. Dawes, and J. Monahan, "Better Decisions Through Science," *Scientific American*, October 2000, 82–87.

22. For a general review of bootstrapping performance, see C. Camerer, "General Conditions for the Success of Bootstrapping Models," *Organizational Behavior and Human Performance* 27, no. 3 (1981): 411–422, which builds on and refines the classic paper by K. R. Hammond, C. J.

Hursch, and F. J. Todd, "Analyzing the Components of Clinical Infer-ence," *Psychological Review* 71, no. 6 (November 1964): 438–456.

23. G. Klein, *The Power of Intuition* (New York: Currency, 2004); and R. M. Hogarth, *Educating Intuition* (Chicago: University of Chicago Press, 2001). See also D. Kahneman and G. Klein, "Conditions for Intuitive Expertise: A Failure to Disagree," *American Psychologist* 64, no. 6 (September 2009): 515–526.

24. P. Goodwin, "Integrating Management Judgment and Statistical Methods to Improve Short-Term Forecasts," *Omega* 30, no. 2 (April 2002): 127–135; for medical examples, see J. Reason, "Human Error: Models and Management," *Western Journal of Medicine* 172, no. 6 (June 2000): 393–396; and B. J. Dietvorst, J. P. Simmons, and C. Massey, "Algorithm Aversion: People Erroneously Avoid Algorithms After Seeing Them Err," *Journal of Experimental Psychology: General* 144, no. 1 (February 2015): 114–126.

25. R. C. Blattberg and S. J. Hoch, "Database Models and Managerial Intuition: 50% Model + 50% Manager," *Management Science* 36, no. 8 (August 1990): 887–899.

26. Related cognitive processes involve associative networks, scripts, schemata, frames, and mental models; see J. Klayman and P. J. H. Schoe-maker, "Thinking About the Future: A Cognitive Perspective," *Journal of Forecasting* 12, no. 2 (1993): 161–186.

27. R. Hastie, S. D. Penrod, and N. Pennington, *Inside the Jury* (Cambridge, MA: Harvard University Press, 1983).

28. J. Klayman and Y.-W. Ha, "Confirmation, Disconfirmation, and Information in Hypothesis Testing," *Psychological Review* 94, no. 2 (April 1987): 211–228; and J. Klayman and Y.-W. Ha, "Hypothesis Testing in Rule Discovery: Strategy, Structure, and Content," *Journal of Experimental Psychology: Learning, Memory, and Cognition* 15, no. 4 (July 1989): 596–604.

29. T. Gilovich, "Something Out of Nothing: The Misperception and Misinterpretation of Random Data," chap. 2 in *How We Know What Isn't So: The Fallibility of Human Reason in Everyday Life* (New York: Free Press, 1991); see also N. N. Taleb, *Fooled by Randomness: The Hidden Role of Chance in Life and in the Markets* (New York: Random House, 2004).

30. The best way to untangle the confounding effects is through controlled experiments, and even then it may be difficult. For a research example of how to do this, see P. J. H. Schoemaker and J. C. Hershey, "Utility Measurement: Signal, Noise, and Bias," *Organizational Behavior and Human Decision Processes* 52, no. 3 (August 1992): 397–424.

31. J. D. Sterman, *Business Dynamics: Systems Thinking and Modeling for a Complex World* (New York: McGraw-Hill, 2000).

32. For textbook introductions to some of these technologies, see J. M. Zurada, *Introduction to Artificial Neural Systems* (St. Paul, MN: West Publishing Company, 1992); and S. Haykin, *Neural Networks: A Comprehensive Foundation*, 2nd ed. (Upper Saddle River, NJ: Prentice-Hall, 1998).

33. "Technology Quarterly: Finding a Voice," *Economist*, January 7, 2017, https://www.economist.com/technology-quarterly/2017-05-01/language/; see also J. Turow, *The Daily You: How the New Advertising Industry Is Defining Your Identity and Your Worth* (New Haven, CT: Yale University Press, 2011).

34. R. Copeland and B. Hope, "The World's Largest Hedge Fund Is Building an Algorithmic Model from Its Employees' Brains," *Wall Street Journal*, December 22, 2016, https://www.wsj.com/articles/the-worlds-largest-hedge-fund-is-building-an-algorithmic-model-of-its-founders-brain-1482423694.

35. "Perspectives on Research in Artificial Intelligence and Artificial General Intelligence Relevant to DoD," JASON Study JSR-16-Task-003, MITRE Corporation, McLean, Virginia, January 2017, https://fas.org/irp/agency/dod/jason/ai-dod.pdf.

36. Prediction banks are a special case of the more general notion of setting up a mistake bank; see J. M. Caddell, *The Mistake Bank: How to Succeed by Forgiving Your Mistakes and Embracing Your Failures* (Camp Hill, PA: Caddell Insight Group, 2013).

37. R. Feloni, "Billionaire Investor Ray Dalio's Top 20 Management Principles," *Business Insider*, November 5, 2014, https://www.businessinsider.com/ray-dalios-bridgewater-management-principles-2014-11.

38. A. Edmondson, "Psychological Safety and Learning Behavior in Work Teams," *Administrative Science Quarterly* 44, no. 2 (June 1999): 350–383.

39. R. S. Michalski, J. G. Carbonell, and T. M. Mitchell, eds., *Machine Learning: An Artificial Intelligence Approach* (Berlin: Springer Verlag, 1983).
40. See, for example, H. Kunreuther, R. J. Meyer, and E. O. Michel-Kerjan, eds. (with E. Blum), *The Future of Risk Management*, under review with the University of Pennsylvania Press.

Chapter 10

1. Authors who have proposed definitions or descriptions of organiza-tion agility or adaptability include S. L. Brown and K. Eisenhardt, *Competing on the Edge: Strategy as Structured Chaos* (Boston, MA: Harvard Business Publishing, 1998); H. W. Volberda, *Building the Flexible Firm: How to Remain Competitive* (New York: Oxford University Press, 1998); D. Sull, *The Upside of Turbulence: Seizing Opportunity in an Uncertain World* (New York: HarperCollins, 2009); S. Haeckel, *Adaptive Enterprise: Creating and Leading Sense-and-Respond Organizations* (Boston: Harvard Business Publishing, 1999); and M. Beer, *High Commitment, High Performance: How to Build a Resilient Organization for Sustained Advantage* (San Francisco: Jossey-Bass, 2009).
2. Researchers who have addressed strategic features of agility include Y. Doz and M. Kosonen, "The Dynamics of Strategic Agility: Nokia's Roller-coaster Experience," *California Management Review* 50, no. 3 (Spring 2008): 95–118; and G. Hamel and L. Välikangas, "The Quest for Resil-ience," *Harvard Business Review* 81, no. 9 (September 2003): 52–63. Researchers exploring agility and adaptability from a design perspective include J. Galbraith, *Designing the Customer-Centric Organization: A Guide to Strategy, Structure, and Process* (San Francisco: John Wiley & Sons, 2011); and C. O'Reilly and M. Tushman, "Organizational Ambidexter-ity: Past, Present, and Future," *Academy of Management Perspectives* 27, no. 4 (November 2013): 324–338. Researchers exploring agility from other perspectives include J. D. Kasarda and D. A. Rondinelli, "Innova-tive Infrastructure for Agile Manufacturers," *Sloan Management Review* 39, no. 2 (Winter 1998): 73–82; S. David and C. Congleton, "Emotional Agility," *Harvard Business Review* 91, no. 11 (November 2013): 125–128; and R. A. Heifetz, A. Grashow, and M. Linsky, *The Practice of Adaptive*

Leadership: Tools and Tactics for Changing Your Organization and the World (Boston: Harvard Business Publishing, 2009).

3. C. G. Worley, T. D. Williams, and E. E. Lawler III, *The Agility Factor* (San Francisco: Jossey-Bass, 2014).

4. J. O'Toole and W. Bennis, "What's Needed Next: A Culture of Candor," *Harvard Business Review* 87, no. 6 (June 2009): 54–61.

5. There are a variety of studies describing capabilities and dynamic capabilities, including S. G. Winter, "Understanding Dynamic Capabilities," *Strategic Management Journal* 24, no. 10 (October 2003): 991–995.

6. W. A. Shewhart, *Economic Control of Quality of Manufactured Product* (New York: Van Nostrand, 1931).

7. The original "freedom and responsibility" document has come under some scrutiny by those who correctly observe that the policies derived from the document apply only to employees who are not involved in the core DVD distribution and streaming business. What these short-sighted observations fail to acknowledge is that these are the missing pieces of planning, organizing, and controlling an "ambidextrous" organization. We know a lot about how to efficiently and effectively manage Netflix's core business (and other similar business models), but we know very little about designing organizations for continuous innovation and change. The "freedom and responsibility" policy provides insights into how to make creativity and innovation routine.

8. I. Barreto, "Dynamic Capabilities: A Review of Past Research and an Agenda for the Future," *Journal of Management* 36, no. 1 (January 2010): 256–280.

9. We adopted methods from Richard Foster, Sarah Kaplan, Anita M. McGahan, and others. See R. Foster and S. Kaplan, *Creative Destruction: Why Companies That Are Built to Last Underperform the Market—and How to Successfully Transform Them* (New York: Random House, 2011); A. M. McGahan, "Competition, Strategy, and Business Performance," *California Management Review* 41, no. 3 (Spring 1999): 74–101; A. M. McGahan, "The Performance of U.S. Corporations: 1981–1994," *Journal of Industrial Economics* 47, no. 4 (December 1999): 373–398; and A. M. McGahan and M. E. Porter, "What Do We Know About Variance in Accounting Profitability?," *Management Science* 48, no. 7 (July 2002): 834–851.

Chapter 11

1. We build on Ron Adner's definition of an ecosystem as a set of relationships involving multiple partners to deliver value to customers. Although Adner thinks of relationships primarily as interdependencies between makers of complements, we think of relationships as alliances, joint ventures, or shorter-term collaborations, irrespective of whether they exist between competitors, suppliers, makers of substitutes, or the makers of complements. See R. Adner, "Ecosystem as Structure: An Actionable Construct for Strategy," *Journal of Management* 43, no. 1 (January 2017): 39–58.

2. In the academic research on interorganizational relationships, a close parallel to a centralized ecosystem is a hub-and-spoke network comprising a broker that works with unconnected partners and benefits from internalizing their knowledge. The academic term for this brokerage strategy is "tertius gaudens." This line of research emphasizes brokerage advantage in the environment when an innovation doesn't require simultaneous mobilization of resources from multiple partners. A tertius gaudens broker takes resources or ideas from its partners and executes on its own. However, emerging research suggests a different, dynamic view on brokerage. That is, a broker can benefit from identifying partners that normally don't work with one another and bringing these partners together. In this strategy, termed "tertius iungens," the broker can create value not only for itself, but also for the partners. For tertius gaudens, see see R. Burt, *Structural Holes: The Social Structure of Competition* (Cambridge, MA: Harvard University Press, 1995); for tertius iungens, See D. Obstfeld, "Social Networks, the Tertius Iungens Orientation, and Involvement in Innovation," *Administrative Science Quarterly* no. 50 (March 1, 2005): 100–130.

3. See Cisco Hyperinnovation Living Lab, assorted videos, n.d., https://vimeo.com.

4. P. Houzé, interview with A. Shipilov, February 2, 2018.

Index